The Solar (

The story of a local church on an incredible adventure of faith

By

Henry Kendal

"This is a remarkable book . . . . It is a gift to the wider church . . . . Henry's book is not for the faint hearted. Each page navigates the twists and turns of the realities of a significant building project, when rooted in a prayerful Godly vision and bucket loads of gumption. This book reveals an ambitious building development, which is ultimately rooted in an enlarged vision of the Kingdom of God, serving the people of North London. But, you have been warned. This is a ministry that has come at a cost, and Henry's helpful first hand reflection is an insightful reminder that such costs are personal and often hidden at the time. Yet, as Henry powerfully shares, all too often our vision is shaped by being risk averse, so it is all the more important that we take time in immersing ourselves on this experience where there has been no attempt to domesticate the wildness of the Spirit, and already so many people have benefitted, particularly in the harshest days of lockdown and Covid 19. Thank you Henry, and thank you St B's."

Rt Revd ROB WICKHAM,
Bishop of Edmonton

"What happens when a church listens to God, dreams big, and isn't intimated by the giants? A remarkable testimony of vision, faith, courage and sacrifice – motivated by a passion to better present Jesus to a community."

PAUL HARCOURT, National
Leader, New Wine England

"An incredible story of vision, faith and perseverance. If you want to increase your vision and faith in a BIG God this is a must read! It has been one of the privileges of my life to see this story of faith and provision unfold."

MIKE PAVLOU, Evangelist and
Church-Planter

"An incredible story of God's provision – read it and increase your faith."

RICHARD GREEVES, Chartered Surveyor and Managing partner of DWD

"We all know the 'church' is people – God's people called to live counter-culturally in every generation, in praise of God and in grace-filled mission to those without faith in Jesus. But His people need to congregate in buildings (especially in cold climates like the UK). Although piles of stone were great memorials to God's faithfulness in leading the Jews into the promised land, church buildings are meant to be continuously adaptable so that they are fit for purpose, both for the worship of God and the mission of God in each new generation. This book is a fascinating story about one church's journey of discovery in hearing and obeying the whisper of the Spirit, to re-locate its building to enable it to minister God's love more effectively in suburban, multi-cultural North London. It's a story about the faith, courage, and generosity of God's people; but above all it's the story of the desire and faithfulness of God in enabling his people to be at the centre of a community's transformation in the 21st Century."

JOHN COLES, Chairman of New Wine and former vicar of St Bs

... like a good detective novel, you know they will succeed in the end but there are moments of torment and many twists and turns on the way. This time a testament to God's wisdom and the power of faith and prayer...."

MARC GOUGEON-RAWCLIFFE, erstwhile architect and St Bs Church Manager

The Solar Option retells a fascinating story of faith with ups and downs and twists and turns in leading a vibrant

Church of England congregation through relocation onto the High Street. The story of listening to God, to God's people, and to expert consultants, while seeking to lead with faith interacting with architects, property developers, local government, church institutions and the local community has many setbacks and delays. These difficulties (told with humour!) yield many treasures of wisdom for leaders."

JOHN S PEACHEY, chairman,
Youth With A Mission (YWAM)
Harpenden, and co-founder
Orphans Know More

"I whole-heartedly commend this book by my friend Henry to you. I lived the events recounted in this tale with him and the team. As I read the draft of the work, I relived the emotions again and again, remembering the giddy faith as we believed God for the, humanly-speaking, impossible task of moving a church from a 100 plus year-old building to the High Road, and the abyss of despair when time after time things threatened to come crashing down. These events changed us all for good. Before, we believed theoretically, but now we know our God is the God of the impossible. Thank you Henry for writing this record of our journey, and I am so grateful for having been able to ride the roller coaster with you! With my prayers that readers will be challenged to trust God for themselves..."

MIKE VAMVADELIS, St Bs
Church Manager for most of the
duration of the project

Preface and Acknowledgements

The process of writing this book has caused me to relive the great adventure of the Go and Grow project. A mission to relocate St Barnabas from its Edwardian birthplace to a new High Road headquarters building, was never going to be easy, but we would have shrunk back in horror had we known the enormity of what we were taking on at the beginning. Time and again I have had to stop writing to marvel at the extraordinary happenings of those tumultuous years. It seems astonishing to me now that we really did do this, like a dream played out in a different realm. Yet this is a real life story, involving heroic exploits by numerous people, who I was privileged to serve alongside. And it is important to remember that all of this would have been completely impossible but for our wonderful God, who provided abundantly for us every step of the way.

Special thanks goes to my St Barnabas co-adventurers: Richard Greeves, Hannah Parker, Sam Markey, Mike Vamvadelis, Franklin Evans, Sarah Restall, Peter Troup and many others. And to our incredible friends in the Diocese of London: Michael Bye, Fr. Luke Miller, Andrew Garwood Watkins, Andy Brooks, Richard Gough, Fr. John Hawkins, +Peter Wheatley, +Rob Wickham, +Richard Chartres and +Sarah Mullally. The tale would not have happened without the team that kept the St Barnabas home fires burning, while some of us were off pursuing wider vision, so special thanks go to our Discipleship Pastor David Brown, our Associate Vicar Colin Brookes, our Church-planters Mike Pavlou and Helen Shannon, and my Assistant Margaret Peach. Colossal love, respect and thanks go to our St Barnabas family, whose astonishing faith, support and generosity made the whole thing possible. I am hugely grateful to Kirstin Taylor for copy editing the manuscript and Ian Mitchell for his amazing cover design. Finally, my love and thanks go to my family: my son Ollie who advised me on publishing and my dear wife Jane, whose careful reading of the manuscript led to numerous improvements and whose cheerful encouragement sustained me through endless hours of writing.

HK 2022

Chapter 1
Arrival

I arrived at St Barnabas on a bright April morning at the tail end of the last millennium. I was there for an interview for the job of Associate Vicar, under the then Vicar John Coles. There were three candidates that day and we had to endure the awkward moments of standing around at coffee breaks eyeing the opposition. As it happened, I knew one of the other candidates, a multi-gifted prodigy who had part-authored the Alpha course. My heart sank as I thought: "I've got no chance; this guy is amazing."

We were shown around the building. As I stepped over the threshold into the towering interior, I sensed the Spirit speaking to me: "You're going to have to do something about the building."

My initial reaction to this sharp prod to my incorporeal senses was: "What? What has it got to do with me? And what on earth could one do about such a building?" The inside of St Barnabas was massive, very fine in its own way, but also quite foreboding. The nudge from the Lord stuck, trapped in my neocortex, puzzling my thoughts. What did it mean? Where would this lead? A panoply of impossibilities flooded my imagination. I tried to put it out of my mind and concentrate on the task in hand: being interviewed. Little did I know at this point the fantastic adventure I was about to embark on that would dominate my life for the next twenty years.

Much to my surprise, after a second interview, I got the job.

Pic 1.1 Interior of St Barnabas, Holden Road.

Chapter 2
Renewal at St Barnabas

The story of St Barnabas is a remarkable tale of God breaking out in unexpected and dramatic ways. How a dying church became a beacon for renewal; intensely impacting the lives of countless people. How that impact then rippled out through church-planting and sent missionaries. The Spirit of God moved and everything He touched seemed to turn to gold.

Pic 2.1 From original fundraising Brochure for St Barnabas (1914).

Built in the Edwardian heyday of the Church of England, St Barnabas had promised to be a haven for vast congregations of the faithful for future generations. St Bs was consecrated just five months before the outbreak of World War I and found itself in a much changed world. The positivity of the Victorian Christians would never fully recover from the tragedy of the Great War, a catastrophe that their faith told them couldn't happen. So, St Barnabas stood like a magnificent horse-drawn carriage at the dawn of the automobile; strangely redundant before it had been fully road-tested. Despite these dismal portents, the church did prosper in the inter-war period, somewhat bucking the trend for the Church of England in the twentieth century. However, St Barnabas' fortunes did not endure indefinitely and by the 1970s and early 80s the church had slipped into inexorable decline. By the time the longstanding vicar Raymond Miller retired in 1981 only a small remnant survived of the once burgeoning congregation.

In 1982 the new fresh-faced vicar, John Coles, arrived at St Barnabas with his young family, aged 31. John came from a solid evangelical background having completed his first curacy at Greyfriars Church in Reading, formerly known as a "black gown church",[1] where the excellence of biblical teaching was renowned. From there he went for his second curacy at Christ Church Clifton in Bristol, a popular student church, also with a strong evangelical tradition.

---

[1] Black Gown churches were where traditionally the preacher would wear a black "Geneva" preaching gown and became renowned as centres of evangelical biblical exposition.

Pic 2.2 John and Anne Coles.

On coming to St Bs, the bishop lowered John's expectations, suggesting that the prospect of managed decline and closure was what lay ahead. John didn't believe him; with cheerful faith and the optimism of youth he was convinced that the simple preaching of the gospel would yield results. Fiercely intelligent, confidently charming and incredibly capable, few would have bet against John prevailing against the dismal odds he was set. Yet the early months of John's tenure as vicar seemed to point to the bishop's shrewd pessimism. The gospel John preached, that had seen such fruit in Reading and Bristol, yielded little in North London.

It was not long before desperation overwhelmed John. The methodology, in which he was trained and believed, wasn't working and this failure rocked his foundations. It was in that place of despondency, when everything seemed hopeless and John felt he had come to the end of himself, that he encountered God in a fresh way. The Holy Spirit flooded into his soul and new life germinated.

Meanwhile, the old guard at St Barnabas had its back against the wall. Despite the palpable inevitability of the waning of the church, a faction was determined to preserve the diminished remains of its former glory. Yet John was now leading St Bs on a new course and not everyone readily embraced this. People left, and in the midst of the maelstrom, the choir walked out en masse. St Bs was teetering. John considered leaving but felt God say that he should remain. At one notable AGM John confirmed his determination to stay on as vicar to an audible groan: "Oh no."

John and his wife Anne started praying for other couples to come and join the church, and little by little they did. Discipleship meetings using ARM's[2] "Saints Alive"[3] material, were focused on exploring the work of the Holy Spirit, took place at the vicarage and a new church community began to emerge. The group was learning to expect God to move in naturally supernatural ways and encouraged by attending John Wimber[4] conferences, the work of the Holy Spirit blossomed. The sick were healed, demons were delivered and the gospel was proclaimed. Many came to faith and still more can trace their spiritual awakening to those days. Soon Sunday congregations were beginning to grow.

---

[2] Anglican Renewal Ministries

[3] Saints Alive was a course often considered to be a pre-cursor to the Alpha course

[4] John Wimber 1934-1997 was a well-known American pastor, who was a founding leader of Vineyard Church and the Church-planting movement. Wimber has been especially influential in UK, over movements like HTB and New Wine.

The growth of St Bs accelerated through the late 80s and 90s. During this time the still relatively small but growing congregation had its first foray into building projects. In a step of faith to accommodate future anticipated growth, the church underwent internal refurbishment and extension. The chancel was reordered with a new platform, new chairs were bought and a room, called "The Pierce Hall" after a benefactor, was built on the South side of the church.

Stirred by what became known as the Toronto Blessing in the mid-90s, St Bs had started church-planting[5] and sending missionaries. Compelled by the wind of the Spirit, the good news of Jesus Christ could not be contained, and what the great missiologist Roland Allen had theorised about: "the spontaneous expansion of the church"[6], was actually happening.

Despite the improvements made in the late 80s and early 90s, the rapid growth of the church began to put strain on the St Bs outdated buildings. St Barnabas was facing an enviable problem; the church needed to expand its inadequate infrastructure.

---

[5] Church-planting had already started prior to the Toronto Blessing, although St Bs sending missionaries is seen by some as a direct consequence of it.

[6] The Spontaneous Expansion of the Church and the Causes that Hinder It by Roland Allen First published in 1927.

Chapter 3
First thoughts about the building

Buildings have always been more than a mere interest to me. I hesitate to call them a passion, because that feels like the wrong language to use of inert objects of human origin. However, there is no doubt that buildings resonate with the way that my brain is wired. From my earliest childhood I had spent long hours daydreaming about property layouts and structural edifices. My father was a civil engineer and I think my mother would've loved to have been an architect, so somewhere it was in the blood. So it was that I came to forge a career in property, as a surveyor and estate agent. After school, I went to college to study 'Valuation and Estate Management' and then qualified as an Associate of the distinguished sounding professional body: The Incorporated Society of Valuers and Auctioneers, later to be subsumed into The Royal Institution of Chartered Surveyors. What I loved so much about this profession, was the creativity; the deal-making and always trying to maximise a property's potential. Yet I found myself constantly coaxed into sales, with its pressurised manipulation and conniving deceit, which I hated. After nearly a decade I threw in the towel and shifted career to something that I considered more noble: the church.

I started at St Barnabas as associate to the then vicar John Coles. John had recently taken over as director of the huge conference and national movement: New Wine, and so had been looking for someone to help carry the load of local church leadership. From day one he was incredibly releasing, giving me levels of responsibility that I felt ill prepared to cope with. Nevertheless, the freedom I felt under his tutelage allowed me to dream big dreams for the church.

I soon discovered that the issues with the building had already been discussed, but with no progress towards a solution. I remember years earlier John Coles and others from St Bs visiting my previous church, St Peter's Harrow. They looked desirously at the major refurbishment and conversion that we had undertaken there in a building not too dissimilar to St Bs, only to conclude that our answer in Harrow would not solve their issues in Finchley.

St Barnabas Church was, in many respects, a very handsome building, particularly inside. It was a large Edwardian gothic edifice with immense stone pillars and a vaulted wooden ceiling, which created a stunning acoustic that went on to be used by various orchestras for recordings. The Architect J.S. Alder was renowned for his churches. As such, St Barnabas was thought of as a fine example of his work, so much so that during our investigations into developing the site the Council for the Care of Churches[7] produced a report on the church

---

[7] The Council for the Care of Churches is an internal Church of England body responsible for historic buildings. The Church of England is in the unenviable position of having around 14,500 listed buildings, more than any other organisation. In order to cope with the sheer volume of listed churches, English Heritage has delegated many of its responsibilities to the Council for the Care of Churches.

building that recommended that it should be considered for listing[8].

As the Council for the Care of Churches is an internal Church of England body, I was extremely disappointed that it seemed to have no perspective whatsoever on the mission of the church. The report didn't even mention the

Pic 3.1 St Barnabas, Holden Road.

vibrancy of the church community at St Barnabas and the need to provide appropriate accommodation for what God was doing here. Instead, it concerned itself purely with bricks and mortar.

---

[8] A listed building in England is one that has special historical or architectural interest and is therefore protected, with restrictions on any alterations or demolition. These listings are administered by English Heritage.

I knew that if the church were listed, we would have great difficulty in pursuing plans for redevelopment, whether those be on-site or elsewhere. We, therefore, commissioned a counter-report, done by a church member and former missionary, David Gurtler. In a tense encounter with the then Archdeacon, I was warned not to go ahead with the counter-report, as it would be deemed a provocative act. We went ahead anyway. David Gurtler was a planning consultant by profession and was very well informed on architectural matters. His 30-page report was thoroughly researched and completely blew apart the Council for the Care of Churches 4-page report. It conclusively demonstrated that, whilst St Barnabas was architecturally fine, it was not rare or unusual. The architect John Samuel Alder was well known for his churches across North London, many of which survive, and some of which are very similar to St Bs. I had the bizarre and rather unnerving experience of going to conduct a wedding in an "Alder" church near Enfield, only to walk into a carbon copy of St Bs. My initial nerves at ministering in new unfamiliar surroundings dissipated, as I immediately knew where everything was. The wedding went without a hitch, not least because the anticipated away match mysteriously transformed into something akin to a home fixture. However, this church had remained in its original condition without the modifications that have disfigured St Bs architectural integrity. Suddenly it was easy to imagine how St Bs must have been back in its primordial days. It seems that in this case, the much-respected Mr Alder saved the effort of new designs by doing a job-lot of churches.

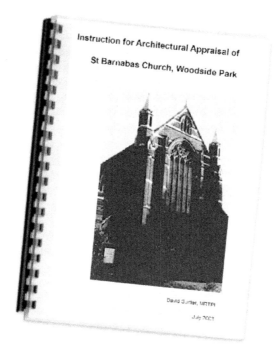

Pic 3.2, David Gurtler's report.

Pic 3.3 Churches by architect John Samuel Alder.

Years later the Council for the Care of Churches position was overruled by yet another obscure church body: The Advisory Board for Redundant Churches (ABRC), vindicating David Gurtler's report. They concluded that the old church was so lacking in merit that they would not object to it being demolished, which in hindsight I actually think is a bit harsh. However, in the years to come we would be grateful that this ruling gave us the liberty to consider all possibilities (including demolition[9]) free of restrictions and free of fear that the building might be listed as an historic monument incapable of alteration.

St Barnabas church was built by visionary pioneers in the early years of the twentieth century, to capitalise on the extension of the Northern Line and the inevitable ensuing population growth. At that time much of the local area was still pastureland, but it would not be long before developments would spring up and new roads, improbably named after Sussex hamlets, would meander along previous sheep trails.

However, by the end of the twentieth century this proud, monolithic structure was beginning to look like an artefact of a bygone age. It had an unwelcoming small narrow entrance and a severe lack of hall space and ancillary accommodation, which made it increasingly unfit for purpose as a modern church. Amazingly, despite its size, it could now barely be seen from any distance, obscured by blocks of flats that had replaced the graceful Victorian and Edwardian villas of yesteryear. The world had moved on, but "the barn" stood impassive to progress, resisting the advent of the modern age.

---

[9] See chapter 10

St Barnabas was a large church building but on a small footprint. At some points, the edge of the plot was only a metre away from the outside of the building, so there was extraordinarily little space for expansion. However, the main sanctuary of the church was quite big, built to accommodate congregations of up to 700. In the 1960s the old church hall in Gainsborough Road was sold off and a new "parish hall" was built inside across the back of the church, there being virtually no space around the outside. This reduced the capacity, but still left an auditorium sufficient for quite large congregations, while providing much needed space for groups.

By the 1990s and with the spectacular growth of the church membership, the building was completely inadequate. The main presenting problem for us, as a church, was one of capacity. With a large and growing congregation, we were running out of space. The main church was near capacity. The toilets, especially the ladies, were inadequate. The kitchen was small and internal. The church offices, that John Coles had moved around to try and find a satisfactory space, were fragmented, dark and too small for a church of our size and growth. One of the biggest problems was the lack of hall space. On Sundays, the 1960s hall at the back of the church was full of children. However, it was the youth who were least provided for, being bussed off-site to a neighbouring church that had an unused hall.

To avoid stunting the growth of the church, something had to be done, and fast. Over my first couple of years, we did two things that proved to be very effective in alleviating the major issues, at least temporarily. Firstly, we craned two prefabricated classroom units onto rented land at the rear of the church, so that the youth could be housed on-site. Secondly, we multiplied our main morning services from one to two, thereby relieving the capacity pressure of just one Sunday morning service. So successful were these strategies that, whilst we only planned for them to persist for just a few years, we ended up continuing to thrive on this site, with only minor modifications, for a further seventeen years. However, the underlying problems had not gone away, with only interim measures in place.

It was in this context that we decided to do a feasibility study into the option of redeveloping the site. The footprint that St Barnabas stood on, being so very tight, meant the necessity for very clever use of the space available if we were to find a way of creating the accommodation we would need.

Marc Rawcliffe, a member of our church and a local architect, drew up some plans. Over the years I have observed that architects generally fall into one of two categories: there are the cool creative ones wearing black collarless T-shirts, jeans and a trendy haircut, and then there are the fuddy-duddy ones who you wonder where they have been these past years. Marc falls firmly into the former category; decidedly cool and creative. On his recommendation, for the past decade, I have become a regular at a particular local barber for my own trendy haircut. Apparently, Marc would have his most inspired moments in the bath, like a latter-day Archimedes getting his eureka epiphany[10]. It is interesting to note that historically architects were often principally

---

[10] Archimedes was a Greek mathematician of antiquity who discovered the displacement of water while in the bath. According to legend he then leapt out of the bath and ran home naked shouting "Eureka!" (I've found it).

mathematicians and scientists, like Isidore of Miletus and Anthemius of Tralles, who designed the astonishing Hagia Sophia in Istanbul, and our very own Sir Christopher Wren, who, when he wasn't building St Pauls Cathedral, was a professor of astronomy and is credited with inventing injections[11]. As an architect, Marc was also one of those out-of-the-box original thinkers who was difficult to pigeonhole; whose cognitive thought trails were always fresh and innovative. Marc, who was soon to also become our part-time church manager, really understood the needs of the church and was therefore the ideal person to do these initial feasibility drawings. The plan he produced involved building a two-storey extension on the embankment at the back of the church, and building permanent tiered seating in the main church, creating a passageway and toilets beneath. Whilst ingenious, the one thing this plan proved was that extending the church on its existing site was not going to be a good option. The redevelopment would be expensive and result in a building with dark passageways and poorly accessible spaces. As is often the case, working with an existing historic building was not proving easy.

The ink was barely dry on Marc's plans when a turn of events changed the landscape. In 2002 the Bungalow next door to the church came on the market. With us struggling to engineer any viable solution to our issues within the tight constraints of our existing site, the opportunity to enlarge our geographical footprint was too good to miss. However, the sale of one small bungalow on a large plot was inevitably going to be for redevelopment

---

[11] In what we would view as a rather cruel experiment, Wren injected alcohol into a dog and watched it become drunk. The rest, as they say, is history.

and we soon found ourselves pitched against an array of seven developers. The distinguished elderly lady who owned the property phoned me and graciously offered to sell the property to St Bs, over the heads of the clamouring cackle of land-hungry speculators, if I would match the best offer. We saw this as the miraculous provision of God for us, but we had to move fast, and such rapidity runs contrary to norms within the Church of England. Parish churches are not empowered to own property in their own right, so normally ownership is vested in the diocese and then nominated to the parish. Unfortunately, the process of getting the diocese to deal can be an arduous one, like waking a sleeping giant from her hibernation. Any prospect of us acquiring this property would need a very quick response, rather than the ponderous machinations of the slumbering diocesan apparatus.

The prospect of being able to acquire this property looked like it would slip through our fingers. I felt frustrated and yet at the same time strangely hopeful. How could we achieve this? It felt so cruel that we were being offered this fantastic opportunity but knew that it was just beyond our reach. We had no money and even if we did, the prescribed means of property acquisition was simply far too slow.

What we needed was a purchase vehicle that could be genuinely fleet-of-foot. Improbably it so happened that, like the Blue Peter catchphrase "here's one I prepared earlier", St Bs had just such a vehicle. The Jesus Kingdom Trust (JKT) was a charity founded ten years previously when relations with the Church of England hierarchy were at such a low ebb that St Bs wanted an instrument through which to continue ministry beyond the jurisdiction of the church authorities, if that became necessary. As a result, the charity was formed, with wide-ranging objects, including the ability to employ people and own property. For a decade, the charity had lain dormant, like a sleeper cell ready to infiltrate foreign territory, and now was its moment. It seemed that God had pre-prepared us for this eventuality.

First, we had to raise some money. A gift day, cobbled together at the last minute, yielded an amazing £150,000, with further interest free loans. Then, with underwriting from the St Bs' Parochial Church Council (PCC), a mortgage offer was obtained. The freshly invigorated JKT sprang into action, I was co-opted onto the trustees, and the bungalow was duly bought for a figure slightly over £½ million. What had looked impossible had happened; the first of many such moments.

With the wind in our sails, we started to dream about the redevelopment on an even larger scale by increasing our footprint still further. The next house along from the bungalow was number 44 Holden Road, an inordinately tall detached late Victorian house with a slightly gothic flavour to it. We affectionately referred to it as the "Addams Family House"[12]. It was in multiple occupancies and was in a slightly dilapidated state. I was keen to find out who owned it. One of our members volunteered to be an amateur sleuth for us and it was not long before she tracked down the name and contact details of the owner. Quite how she did this I did not know and didn't ask. The owner, Mr Joseph Ackerman, was a well-known, fabulously rich, residential landlord owning countless

---

[12] The Addams family is a hugely successful American gothic comedy about a family with macabre goings-on. The franchise included several blockbuster films.

tenement blocks across North London. Apart from having a large property portfolio, he had a reputation for never selling. Nevertheless, heart in mouth, I phoned him up.

In a previous life, when I was an up-market estate agent, making cold calls was a regular feature of work and not something I baulked at. I remember one occasion somehow getting the number of the reclusive Max Factor[13] mogul, Leonard Matchan, who lived on the islet of Brecqhou off Sark in the Channel Islands. I had heard that the elderly hermit-like millionaire was preparing to sell the island[14] and I wanted to persuade him that I was the man for the job. In this instance I failed, but I still made the call. Twenty years on I was not so bold with Joseph Ackerman, but I still made the call.

I was surprised to get straight through to Mr Ackerman, as such people are often notoriously difficult to contact directly. I said that St Bs was interested in buying his house in Holden Road and he responded that he might be interested in buying our church. I said that we could talk about that, to which he laughed; it seemed that my audacity had softened him. In the end, as expected, we made no headway with Mr Joseph Ackerman. I noticed that the house was later substantially

---

[13] Legend has it that Matchan was responsible for the development of roll-out lipstick, although I am unable to corroborate this. He does not even appear in the history of Max Factor on Wikipedia, which either means I am mistaken, or that he somehow blotted his copybook with them and has been duly expunged from their corporate memory. What is not in doubt is that he was hugely wealthy and liked his own company.

[14] In the end Leonard Matchan died before Brecqhou went on the market and as happens with complex estates, it was some years before the island eventually sold, to the Barclay brothers who remain there to this day, much to the chagrin of the other tenants of Sark.

refurbished, and I heard from one of the tenants that it had become a very pleasant place to live. In the last couple of years, subsequent to St Bs' move to the High Road, the house has been demolished and replaced by luxury flats startlingly similar to the much bigger development of St Barnabas next door, so my dream of incorporating this house into the wider St Bs site was not so barmy after all.

The purchase of the bungalow was a triumph, a miraculous divine intervention that was of huge value to us. And yet it didn't really change the realities we faced on the ground. Whilst we now had a larger plot to potentially develop, the same issues around converting and developing an historic church building still remained. No amount of land would eradicate the design compromises we had encountered in Marc's drawings. So, we started to entertain the previously unthinkable idea, the nuclear option: what if we relocated the church and started from scratch?

Chapter 4

An historical assessment of church buildings

Before I continue our story, let me take a chapter to think more deeply about church buildings. It is fair to ask the question: does it require buildings for the church to continue to prosper?

Church buildings have often taken on an importance way beyond their usefulness to the kingdom. I have recently returned from Rome where I visited the colossal St Peter's Basilica that took 200 years and dozens of Popes to complete. The result is an extraordinary edifice that is, at the same time, a magnificent shrine to the glory of God and a formidable statement of the power of the church. One can't help feeling that such a building has moved us a long way from our Christian origins. The fact that, often, when we talk about "a church," we are referring to a building, is a testament to how distracted we have become from the work of the real church – the community of faith. How would the wandering carpenter from Nazareth, with his bunch of burly fishermen followers, react to this monumental architecture of gold and marble? Yet, it has not always been this way.

The church, founded by Jesus, flourished for three hundred years of continuous growth, in the teeth of intense persecution, without a single dedicated building. People met in houses, some of which were adapted to include a chapel. We see this already happening in the

New Testament where we read that Philemon[15] has a church meeting in his home. We also have archaeological evidence of this early church practice from Lullingstone Villa in Kent, built during the Roman occupation in the 1st century; it was later extended to include a Christian chapel.

The advent of church buildings only really came under Constantine the Great in the fourth century. This coincided with what many regard as the church's first major loss of vibrancy. Up until that point the gospel had spread far and wide without the help of organised evangelistic campaigns. The whole trajectory of the church was evangelistic; the gospel was written through it like Brighton rock. It is estimated that each generation of the sub-apostolic early church added about half a million additional new believers, up until by the conversion of Constantine in 312AD when approximately 5-8%[16] of the population of the Roman Empire were born again. However, once the Emperor declared himself a Christian, every ambitious member of the ruling classes would follow suit in order to ingratiate themselves with the hierarchy. A church characterised by courageous persecuted zealots, soon transformed into one full of aspiring sycophantic officials of the Roman government. The once radical, counter-cultural, grassroots movement, soon became a lethargic behemoth of the establishment.

We form our buildings, but then somehow the process is reversed, and our buildings start to form us. We were formed from the earth and the earth is our home; we are people deeply attached to place. We are inevitably

---

[15] Philemon 1:2
[16] Ramsey MacMullen quoted in Wolfgang Simson, Houses that change the world, 1999 page 41.

influenced and affected by our environment, an environment that we have largely built ourselves. It has often been commented that the young radical firebrand politicians who stir support to a fever pitch on the hustings, commonly mellow, becoming more compliant once they enter the hallowed corridors of the Palace of Westminster. Is it possible that the sheer potency of the surroundings, their history, their culture, infiltrates the very hearts of the new incumbents to the point that they become meek in the face of such nobility?

The same dynamic happens to an even greater extent in church buildings, as infrastructure and theology coalesce. Who of us has not been overawed when visiting a magnificent cathedral? I well remember the first time I entered the Hagia Sophia in Istanbul. So vast is this domed 6th century cathedral[17] that birds freely fly around inside. I walked around dumbfounded, gazing upwards in wonderment; utterly overwhelmed by the majesty of this stunning sanctuary. The light, the space, the atmosphere lifted my spirit to worship. If a mere building can do this to our souls, we need to take care lest we build something that points less to God and more to ourselves, for that would be blasphemy.

Church buildings have always reflected the prevailing theology of the day. The first dedicated church buildings started appearing in the fourth century under Constantine

---

[17] The Hagia Sophia was built as the orthodox Christian Cathedral to rival Rome. It was subsequently turned into a mosque by the Ottomans and largely forms the blueprint for mosques built since. In the twentieth century the Hagia Sophia became a secular museum up until July 2020, when Turkey's President Erdogan ordered its reclassification as a mosque. Agonisingly it still remains the symbolic centre of the Greek Orthodox Church, six centuries after it fell to the Ottomans.

the Great. With Christianity now becoming the religion of the state, it became necessary to have some infrastructure to accommodate the church in these new circumstances. No church buildings had existed before and so a new form of architecture had to be invented. When looking at the design of the new buildings the church at that time did a very interesting thing. Nothing ever happens in a vacuum, and one would have expected the new architects of church buildings to draw on the religious architecture of the day – temples. But they didn't. Instead, they took the secular civic building as their template – the Roman Basilica. The pagan temples of the day were closed off buildings centred on the shrine to the god and largely restricted to priests undertaking their oblations away from the gaze of the public. Few people entered them, but instead gathered around outside. In contrast, basilicas were the towns' civic centre, where people would gather, and the magistrate would sit. They were large open buildings full of light and space to mingle; to meet friends and to be seen. This was the model for the new church buildings, so much so that the church went on to call them basilicas.

No Christian had ever worshipped like this before, where one could be part of the throng, mingling with a cacophony of music, words, processions and colour. This harked back to some elements of the Jewish Temple worship[18], which the early church in the first chapters of Acts had engaged. Whilst the teaching and community

---

[18] Much of the Jewish temple worship was centred around animal sacrifice, and this has never been a feature of Christian worship. However, temple worship also included choirs and processions and large gatherings of people, and these elements were adopted by the Christians.

Pic 4.1 Hagia Sophia, Istanbul.

element of church worship traced its roots from the Jewish synagogue[19], up until the time of Constantine the church had been an oppressed minority often worshipping in secret. To be able to openly worship in a bright commodious space must have been a wonderful release from the claustrophobia of the persecuted church that had even occasionally resorted to clandestine worship in the catacombs[20]. The best remaining example of this type of church building is the spectacular basilica of Santa Sabina in Rome. Built 422-432AD, it has been restored largely to its original 5th century layout[21]. I was thrilled to visit Santa Sabina in 2019, enjoying its glorious light and space.

Of course, there was also a negative subtext to the adoption of basilicas as the template for the new churches. Clearly the Roman authorities were making a power play for the church to be integrated into the apparatus of the state, so what better way than to house the church in buildings that looked suspiciously like town halls, rather than select temples. Nevertheless, the church at the time was also making a theological statement that worship was to be open and accessible for everyone, in the same way that the grace of God through the cross of our Lord Jesus Christ is a free gift open to anyone.

Through the centuries, church architectural styles have so often reflected the current mood in theology of that day. So, through the Middle Ages, the great cathedrals were built higher and longer than ever before. The architectural

---

[19] See Wolfgang Simson, ibid, page xv.

[20] This is the origin of the term "underground church".

[21] The only major later augmentation still in the church is the 9th century choir (schola cantorum), but this has low walls and so it is easy to imagine what it was like before this addition.

message reinforced the theology of the glory of God, who is high and lifted up. However, it also conveyed the subtle message that God is a long way away and not approachable. This was further reinforced by the abomination of the "rood[22] screen," a wall or barrier dividing the nave, where the people would gather for worship, and the choir, where the priests, musicians and dignitaries would sit. Again, this was laden with meaning.The ordinary sinners are kept out of the presence of God, while the special people came into the holy of holies. The rood screen was nothing short of a rebuilding of the old covenant temple veil, a barrier to separate us from God, that has been torn from top to bottom at the moment of Jesus death[23]. The church had allowed the old covenant to re-impose itself, virtually obliterating the wonderful grace of the new covenant and annulling Jesus' triumphal work on the cross. To add insult to injury the pulpit was placed out in the nave with the people. So, a priest would deign to make his way out of the glorious panelled cordoned off choir, to come and tell the riff-raff what sinners they were. Meanwhile, his fellow priests sitting up in the choir would not be able to hear his worthy words, presumably as their holiness meant that they didn't need a sermon on repentance. Jesus' "blind guides" rant against the Pharisees in Matthew comes to mind[24].

---

[22] 'Rood' is a middle English word for Cross.

[23] Matthew 27:51. The Mishnah (codified oral law of early rabbinic literature) states that the temple veil was as thick as a man's hand (about 4in or 10cm). As such it was more of a curtain-wall than a flimsy veil.

[24] Matthew 23:13-26.

Pic 4.2 Santa Sabina, Rome.

However, not all church building traditions have been negative. The wonderful uniquely English style

Perpendicular[25], an elaboration on the European gothic, is gloriously light and fresh. Through advances in construction techniques that dramatically reduced the size and mass of window mullions, Perpendicular achieved previously unattainable light and space, which is truly inspiring. Then the post-reformation churches of London, rebuilt after the great fire by Wren, Hawksmoor and others, were probably inspired by the wonderful Perpendicular buildings of their forebears. These famous

Pic 4.3 Lady Chapel, Ely Cathedral.

late 17th to early 18th century architects largely dispensed with the cruciform layout, the towering gothic remoteness and suffocating oppression of the rood screen, to create light airy open churches perhaps even slightly reminiscent

---

[25] Probably the best examples of Perpendicular to be seen today are at Kings College chapel Cambridge and the Lady Chapel at Ely Cathedral.

of the wonderful Santa Sabina built 1300 years earlier. How things come around!

The architectural tug-of-war between something built to express reverence and awe, versus a style that conveys more of the immanence of God, continues to this day. The 19th century saw the Oxford Movement, endorsing more veneration in worship, and at the same time church buildings returned to dark, mysterious, lofty, gothic, now with a Victorian twist. In the 20th century the trend swung again. There is no better place to see this theological-architectural pendulum swing than in Liverpool. The city's two great cathedrals were both built in the 20th century. Taking most of the century to build, the Anglican Cathedral is an astonishing stone structure that feels like it comes from a previous epoch, and from a distance looks as though it could have been there for a millennium. This is gothic at is zenith. It is dark and tall and God is glorious but remote. In contrast, the post-war Roman Catholic cathedral was rapidly constructed in concrete after post-war austerity put paid to more ambitious plans. It is octagonal and accessible. Like King Arthur and his round table, the message is clear. The kingdom of God is close and available - this is the democratisation of faith.

Pic 4.4 Liverpool's two Cathedrals.

More recently a new trend has emerged in church buildings, that of repurposing secular buildings. The converted warehouse is now a feature in church architecture, and even when these churches are purpose-built, some lengths are taken to make them as plain as a warehouse. Many of these new churches have a sanctuary without windows, taking their lead from the theatre rather than an ecclesiastical style. As such they are in danger of reinforcing the tendency towards consumer church, where the congregation becomes an audience watching a show, and the churchgoer does not engage in the community any more than the theatregoer. However, on the positive side, these new churches have managed to dispense with much of the ecclesiastical baggage that was hugely off-putting for many people. By repurposing a secular building or constructing one that looks like a secular building, the new churches stand in the tradition of the early post-Constantinian basilicas. Instead of insisting the people come into a sacred space that is utterly foreign to their everyday lives, the new churches have created spaces so accessible that people barely realise they are in a "church." In the missional setting of the post-Christian West, it is necessary that we go to where people are, rather than expect them to come to us and as such our buildings need to adapt.

Buildings have so often in church history been more of a distraction to the spiritual verve of the church, than a net asset. They are never neutral and are always giving off subliminal messages that either undergird or undermine our theology. Buildings play their part and, in the manner that the western church is currently formulated, good buildings can hugely benefit the mission of the church. They are also all-consuming, expensive, and divisive. So, it is tempting not to bother and simply make do with inadequate facilities. Yet, with all the inherent dangers, attempting to address building issues can be fruitful in the long term. However, the potential for church buildings to take over as the principal determining factor in the vision trajectory of the church is enormous and difficult to avoid. It is dispiriting to acknowledge that in the direction that many churches take, often the building-tail wags the mission-dog. This dog-tail tussle was to become our daily struggle as we at St Bs tried to engage with our infrastructure challenges.

Chapter 5
Years of exploration and frustration

As John Coles' associate, I had come to St Barnabas, at least in part, to learn from him; to sit at his feet. John was (and is) one of the most anointed church leaders of his generation, so to work closely with John and be mentored by him was a dream come true. I imagined years of working quietly in the background under John's direction, learning from him and thereby being equipped for whatever challenge God had in store for me at some point in the future. However, learning is rarely achieved by sitting on the side-lines objectively observing, and it certainly wasn't going to be that way for me. Almost immediately I was plunged into the deep end of church leadership, leadership that included the pressing need to address our buildings. We inevitably faced, not just the intractable problems of an inadequate building to accommodate us, but with it the danger of distraction from the work of the kingdom by needing to address those problems. This was the highway of hazards that I stepped onto just before the turn of the millennium.

Fairly early on in our deliberations, we set up a "building development group" chaired by Franklin Evans, a member of the church and a barrister in a slightly Rumpolian style with a prodigious legal brain and an erudite and witty turn of phrase. The group was tasked with exploring all options and reporting to the PCC.

Having taken the radical step of turning down the prospect of redeveloping the existing church, we started to cast around for an alternative site. Immediately one presented itself that felt like a real possibility. And it was on our doorstep.

We had already leased land from Transport for London (TFL) round the back of the church. This was where we had craned in two second-hand prefabricated classroom units, and later would add a metal framed youth hall, a portacabin type office and build a large conservatory to bridge the gap between the other prefabricated buildings. This group of buildings would go on to serve us well for a decade and a half, providing much needed space for our burgeoning youth ministry, as well as extra office accommodation. Whilst all temporary, the whole thing would become quite an encampment, with its own bespoke pathway and attractive external decking area. At its height about 15 staff were working in these temporary buildings.

The patch of land we rented was only a small portion of the TFL land that ran adjacent to the Northern Line. Immediately adjacent to our plot was a larger site that extended to the turn-around in front of Woodside Park station. Around 2004 the idea came to build a new church there in front of the station. In London it is quite common for the entrance to underground stations to be incorporated into a shopping centre or another public building. So, we thought: why not a church? Transport for London would get a renewed entrance to Woodside Park Station and we in turn would get a new church building as the highly visible entrance to the station. Marc Rawcliffe had drawn up some sketches for a spectacular church centre that would share its entrance with the station. The building would be on several floors, capped off with a beautiful light and airy main sanctuary on the top floor. I was excited by the prospect of this building providing for all our needs, with a fresh innovative design. Surely God would make a way for us to achieve our goal.

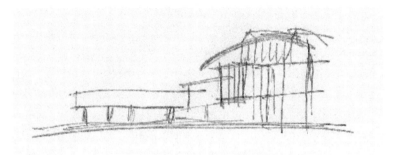

Pic 5.1 Marc's sketch elevation.

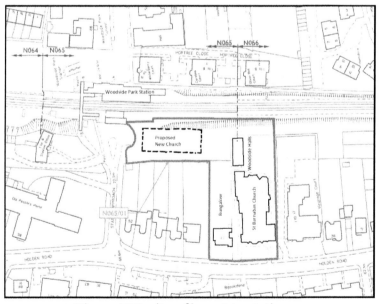

Pic 5.2 TFL site adjacent to station.

We went into negotiations with TFL's property department. TFL is quite a large landowner, albeit predominantly in long narrow strips. Letters were written; emails were exchanged, and visits were made to their offices in Victoria. Initially they seemed interested in the prospect of us developing on their land and so we were encouraged to push forwards.

However, it soon became clear that this was not an easy organisation to deal with. As with other quasi-governmental monolithic bureaucracies, getting an answer out of TFL seemed to be virtually impossible. The organisation was opaque. It was rare that they would answer within even a few months, and by that time the person who you had been dealing with, with whom you thought you were building some kind of relationship, had moved on and a new face had arrived wanting to print his or her authority on the matter. We laboured on in this way for years, always with sufficient hope that just around the corner the answer would come. And so we kept trying.

Eventually, having made no discernible progress, we got in touch with an illustrious Christian Surveyor named Henry Clarke, famed for forging deals, particularly with railway companies. Henry was ebullient about our chances and so, with what would surely be the one last attempt, we pressed our case. The result was that at last a decision would be made. Our proposal that TFL should sell this patch of land to us to enable St Bs to build a new church centre, was to be put to "mayor's opinion". In order to avoid different departments pursuing contradictory strategies, certain decisions were designated to be taken at the highest level, where all aspects of TFLs future schemes could be taken into consideration. The scheme would be put to the mayor's office, with representation of other TFL stakeholders. We were now in the hands of the then mayor: Boris Johnson.

Pic 5.3 Ian Mitchell's cartoon in church magazine.

The wait was interminable. Many prayers were lifted over those months: "Please God open up the way ahead". Finally, the news came through in April 2009. The mayor had refused permission to release the land. The reason cited was that this land had been designated for use as a depot to facilitate the upgrading of the Northern Line. I was devastated. We had worked tirelessly for five years to try and achieve our dream. Where was God in this? All those wasted years, with nothing to show for our efforts. I was filled with frustration that such a simple decision had taken so long. In the snakes and ladders world of the property market we had been caught by the devil's snake, and now we were back to square one. But at least we had certainty, and now we could move on.

The High Road

So it was that we started to turn our attention towards looking for a site on the North Finchley High Road. Perhaps the main problem with this was the constraints of our parish. The Church of England is a deeply geographical organisation. In generations past the church had been formulated on the assumption that England was a Christian country. What does one do with a Christian country? – one pastors it. To do this effectively the Church of England parcelled up the entire country into around 12600 parishes, roughly one for each village sized area. Each of these parishes has a church building at its centre and a vicar to pastor the flock[26]. This system has served the church well and has many advantages to it: the whole country is in some way covered; difficult areas are not ignored, and it keeps things local and personal.

In recent times there has been an acknowledgement that the Church of England no longer presides over a predominantly Christian country, but that we find

---

[26] Many rural areas now have to share a single vicar across a number of parishes.

ourselves in an unmistakeably missional situation. This has given rise to many exciting new strategies like church-planting, pioneer ordained ministry and resource churches. However, the structure of the parish system is still the backbone of the Church of England. In the past the rigidity of these demarcations has been stultifying to growth. Bishop David Pytches famously described the parochial system as "the condom of the Church of England", preventing natural reproduction. And there is no doubt that we at St Barnabas were feeling the constricting pressure of our parish boundary straight-jacket. There were very few prospective sites anywhere in our small parish. Specifically, our parish only encompassed a short section of one side of the North Finchley High Road. The options were extremely limited.

However, there was one possible site – the council's Lodge Lane Car Park. So, in the summer of 2009 we drafted a plan to build a new shopping centre on the site, with an attractive central atrium, plenty of parking to replace the surface car park, and a church and other facilities on the upper floors. This was not just a church plan, but a catalyst for the regeneration of the North Finchley Town Centre. I went to see the leader of the council Mike Freer[27] who had asked the then head of planning Martin Cowey to join us. Ever the politician, Mike seemed to understand our predicament and was keen to try and help us find a solution. He pointed to Martin, saying that this was the man who would help us and in turn Martin sounded very positive.

---

[27] Mike Freer is now MP for Finchley and Golders Green.

Pic 5.4 Parish map: thick line outlines St Barnabas parish and faint line outline parish of St John's Whetstone.

I had already been at St Barnabas nearly a decade and from the perspective of the building project, so far had nothing to show for it. I was beginning to become more realistic about our prospects. Sure enough, once the meeting was over and away from the sight of his political master, Mr Cowey became far less obliging and instead started to point out the shortcomings in our plan.

To be fair the Lodge Lane Car Park has long been a political hot potato. It was and is clearly an underdeveloped piece of land in the heart of an area of North London that suffers from quite extreme pressures on space; so why not develop it? Unfortunately, the site has a history of people becoming very defensive and suspicious about any proposal to develop it. Fearful that North Finchley will lose its one decent-sized car park, the Lodge Lane lobby is a powerful voice for retaining the status quo.

With our champion Mike Freer, elevated by the electorate to the office of MP and heading off to Westminster, it became clear that Barnet was not going to do anything with the Lodge Lane Car Park site in the foreseeable future. Having been burnt by fruitless years of negotiations with TFL, I wasn't in any mood to repeat such purgatory with another equally impervious arm of government, the London Borough of Barnet.

However, one positive outcome of the Lodge Lane discussions with Barnet, was that we had come to realise that a High Road location was a top priority for us. If we were to achieve our objectives, we would need a whole lot of highly improbable things to fall into place. This was to be a walk of faith, far more than a property transaction. But we would need to, not only be full of faith, but also professionally savvy in the ruthless world of property development; "as wise as serpents and as innocent as doves"[28]. Up until that point, we had only been following our noses, taking the next step presenting itself right in

---

[28] Matthew 10:16.

front of us. If a way ahead had opened up, this would have worked well, but in fact, after a decade of graft, we had got nowhere. So now, through prayer, we started to be far more intentional about the way we approached the project. We laid the whole future of the church before the Lord and came up with fourfold "guiding principles" for why we wanted to take the so-called nuclear option of relocating the church.

The guiding principles were:

1. The current building is functionally obsolete.

The presenting reasons for this obsolescence were
   a) We were at capacity on Sundays. Over the years we had tried to mitigate the effect of this space saturation, e.g., multiplying the services (we no longer had another easy time to multiply again); planting churches (being a recurrent planting church generally requires a larger hub parent church, so planting doesn't necessarily alleviate the problem).
   b) We had inadequate halls and offices.
   c) We were totally dependent on temporary buildings and temporary planning consents on rented land.
   d) The building was old and inefficient.
The implications of this were that tinkering around the edges would not suffice and a completely new-build would be preferable.

2. Ministry is more important than buildings.

This being the case we should not focus on the buildings to the degree that the ministry is badly impeded in the process. I confess I was very worried by almost every aspect of the project. At one point we considered redeveloping on our existing site, but apart from the disadvantage of remaining in a back road, the plan would involve the prospect of relocating the entire church for 15 months. Of course, there may have been ways of phasing the redevelopment to lessen this, but nevertheless the disruption would have been phenomenal. I think I would have needed to almost hear the audible voice of God before embarking on such a massive interruption. There was a real danger that we might build a beautiful new church facility only to have killed the church in the process.

There are myriad examples of churches that have overly focussed on getting the right building whatever the cost and ended up decimated. I once visited a massive Pentecostal church in Sweden that had undertaken a huge new-build construction project. The result was a church centre so lovely that I am still tempted to covet my neighbour's church. Fifteen years on I remember almost every aspect of it: it had a fabulous 800 seat sanctuary and a very attractive cosy 120 seat chapel in the loft. The senior pastor's office was like that of a major company CEO: desk at one end, sofa area at the other, with picture windows overlooking the town's river. However, during the construction project, the church went through a disastrous split. Much of the congregation left and the now much smaller church found themselves encumbered with a massive building. I visited shortly after the building was finished. They were not using the main sanctuary but instead met on Sundays in the ground floor café.

The tragic tale of that Swedish church is a salutary reminder not to get enticed into overly ambitious building projects while neglecting the more important matter of the health of the church.

3. We want to spend the least we can on buildings, preferring mission expenditure.

Our main focus for our expenditure is and always should be mission. I remain alarmed at the way some churches spend incredible amounts of money on buildings, out of proportion with their ministry and mission. I remember once standing in an African field chatting to a Kenyan bishop about his ambitious plans for a new cathedral and discipleship centre. He commented on how he didn't understand the mentality of churches in the West that spent such vast sums on themselves, often with little to show for it, while an investment of a fraction of that would yield incredible fruit in his setting. I had no repost; embarrassed I simply looked at the ground and wondered if I had got everything wrong. Whilst saying this, I realise that this was the trap that we at St Bs were inexorably heading towards, somehow lured by the irresistible logic of the need for a decent building. Of course, it is right to spend appropriately on buildings – I only question the amount. So, I set it as my objective to find a way of getting us a good facility at an affordable amount. It is an ambition that I am not convinced we achieved, but the intention was there.

Quite apart from the probity of spending huge sums, I also did not think it was achievable. Whilst our people were incredibly generous, unlike some churches, we didn't have a tranche of super-rich to bankroll us. I didn't want to lack faith, but there did need to be an element of realism.

My original strategy was to trade a valuable residential site where we were in Holden Road, for a less valuable tertiary commercial site, to give us a financial leg-up. Others quickly critiqued this, pointing out that it didn't stack up because even if residential sites have high values, commercial property is generally far more expensive both to build and to maintain. Additionally, the site swap strategy would massively increase the complexity of the project, with the unescapable implication of increased costs.

4. A back-road location is not ideal

We identified that there were two compelling motivations for locating our church.

a) As a large regional hub church, we would like good communications and parking (we were previously near the tube and you could park reasonably easily nearby), but also somewhere highly visible (our current location made us largely invisible).

b) As a church involved in local mission, we would like to be in the centre of the town, which is often a location with difficult parking restrictions – hence the conflict.

Our current location was, when judged against these objectives, falling a long way short. Yes, we had good access to a tube station and reasonable parking, albeit at the cost of inconveniencing our Holden Road neighbours, but the big problem was the back-road hiddenness of St Bs. Astonishingly for such a large building St Bs was hardly visible in the townscape. You had to be practically right in front of it to see it, and once you were a couple of houses away it was obscured by trees and roofs, as if it never existed. Added to that, Holden Road, being a quiet, leafy residential road, had virtually no passing trade and you needed a good SatNav to find us. Therefore, we were battling with the tendency to become like a private club for those in the know, because visitors would have trouble finding us. From a strategic overview of North London, we weren't really on the map. It is amazing that God had grown such a large church in such a concealed location.

The only properly suitable location for a church of our size was on the High Road. The North Finchley High Road is part of the Great North Road, the principal Roman route of communication from Londinium (London) to York, the North and Scotland. It was the Roman HS2 and an equally astonishing feat of engineering. It is the stuff of Dick Turpin legends and Walter Scott novels. Today much of the original route of the Great North Road is followed by the A1, but in our part of the London Borough of Barnet the road is denominated by the A1000. It remains a major artery of communication for London with 56,000 people travelling on it through North Finchley each week.

———————

Now, having abandoned all hope of the Lodge Lane site ever being available to us, we had exhausted the only conceivable option of a High Road site within our parish. The parish of St Barnabas Woodside Park had originally been carved out of the more northerly outreaches of the parish of Christ Church North Finchley sometime in the late nineteenth century as London expanded and the new population needed new churches to provide for them. However, having been formed out of pre-existing boundaries, it was not only geographically small, but also rather peculiarly shaped. One of the parish's idiosyncrasies is that it only includes a very short stretch of one side of the High Road. There seemed to be little prospect of relocating the church on to the High Road within the constraints of the Church of England's parochial structure.

Nevertheless, more by blind faith than logic, we continued to look for potential sites. Richard Greeves a Chartered Surveyor and commercial agent, who was and is a member of St Bs, had volunteered to help in the search. Some while earlier Richard had been attending St Bs one Sunday morning when the service leader Colin Brookes[29] announced: "there's someone here called Richard who wants to get more involved at St Bs". Richard responded to this divine call by speaking to me after the service and was promptly drafted into the building development group. Richard is a gregarious, ebullient man with many years of experience as a dealmaker. He had put his sociability to good use constantly entertaining clients, being known affectionately to his office colleagues as "Sir Lunch-a-lot",

---

[29] Colin was St Bs' Associate Vicar

and as a result was very well connected in the property world. Richard tirelessly trawled through the property pages to unearth the illusive site for our new church.

Then a series of three incidents in quick succession happened to me that changed my perspective.

The first encounter happened while I was attending a clergy day at St Marys Edgware, which was at the time an Anglican abbey and convent. When, in between sessions wandering down the cloister, I bumped into the Archdeacon, he commented something about the adjacent parish to us having its living suspended[30]. When I looked blank, he realised that he had divulged too much information and quickly backtracked. However, I couldn't un-know what I had heard, and I pondered what it might mean.

The second encounter was later that day, when I was giving a lift home to our neighbour, the incumbent of St Johns Whetstone, Revd Kevin Mitchell; he confided in me that he was taking early retirement and that an announcement was to be made soon. I quickly put two and two together and realised that it must be St Johns' living that was to be suspended after Kevin's departure. At the time St Johns was a small Anglo-Catholic church parish, which had struggled financially over quite a long period of time, and it was now clear that they couldn't afford the cost of having a new vicar after Kevin retired.

The third occurrence was when I got home, and I looked at my emails. There I found several emails from Richard Greeves. Richard had unearthed several potential sites on the High Road, but none of them were in our

---

[30] The "living being suspended" means that a church is not fully viable and as a result will no longer get a paid-for vicar.

parish. Indeed, a couple of them were in the parish of St Johns Whetstone. In our discussions I had made it very clear to Richard that any site had to be within the geographical parish of St Barnabas. So, as I looked at the property details Richard had forwarded to me, I became rather irritated. I was about to write a curt reply email pointing out his mistake, and could he please be more diligent by keeping the search to within the parish in future. But then I stopped dead in my tracks.

First the Archdeacon, then the neighbouring vicar, and then Richard's emails. I suddenly realised that God was saying something to me. Was it possible that God would open up a way for us to relocate our parish church into another parish? Had such a thing ever happened before in the Church of England?! It is hard to overestimate the grip that the parish structure has on the collective Church of England psyche. Along with belief in the Holy Trinity[31] and the approbation of the 1662 Book of Common Prayer, there is no higher creed than the venerated English parish. But with these three incidents I felt that I should at least explore the potential of breaking the shackles of our parish. I booked to see the bishop.

Our local area Bishop, Rt Revd Peter Wheatley, had become a friend to St Barnabas. Previously St Bs had been such an aberration to the norm in the Church of England that the church's hierarchy had been very suspicious of us. But +Peter had embraced our distinctive flavour, with all

---

[31] There are those in the Church of England whose belief in the Trinity has appeared to have wavered, perhaps more than their adherence to the parish structure. However, the doctrine of Trinity remains the heart of the catholic creeds recited in Church of England churches weekly.

Pic 5.5 Bishop Peter Wheatley at St Barnabas.

its signs of life and growth and had always given the appearance of loving his visits to us for confirmations[32] and other official ceremonies. +Peter was an Anglo-Catholic single man approaching retirement. His churchmanship was, in practically every way, the diametric opposite of St Bs, and so whilst he graciously embraced us, he never really understood us. He once told me that he had rationalised that we were in effect a youth church. St Bs was of course not a youth church, but perhaps this description helped +Peter pigeonhole us and thereby know how to treat us.

Despite +Peter being a kindly pastoral man, I entered his office that day with great trepidation. I could not think of a more radical request to make than to propose moving a parish church into someone else's parish. In my mind, I might as well be confessing some heinous sin or asking if the bishop was happy for me to become an atheist. As I started to explain, I was aware of a nervous tremor in my voice and the dread of the moment left me unable to prevent my legs from shaking. Once I had made my pitch, without hesitation, the bishop smilingly responded: "my dear boy, of course, go ahead, don't worry I'll sort out the legal issues". I couldn't believe it. Utterly dumbstruck and still shaking with nervous tension, waves of relief and joy flooded my mind and body. Here was the most law-abiding of bishops tearing up the rulebook for a church far removed from his own ecclesiastical preference! He was not just giving me permission; he was positively

---

[32] Confirmation in the Church of England is the rite of the laying on of hands by a bishop for the impartation of the Holy Spirit. It is entered into as an adult choice and is used to confirm baptism, particularly for those who were baptised as infants.

encouraging me. I was stupefied by what God was doing through the most unlikely channels.

Chapter 6
Site or sight

After getting the Bishop's permission, we started to look in earnest for an appropriate High Road site. The vast majority of the High Road near St Bs parish was in the parish of St Johns Whetstone, that being a very long narrow parish; a ribbon encompassing nearly a mile of both sides of the High Road. The fact that St Johns was at the time a parish in suspension, probably strengthened our case for doing something in that area. And so, with new-found confidence, we began to seriously investigate potential sites.

The first site that presented itself as a possible option, was in fact a double site. It was two adjoining pieces of land in different ownerships on the High Road, opposite an Audi garage and backing onto a golf course and tennis club. We went to visit the developer Dorchester Group and their chief executive Gary Silver. Gary assured us that both portions of the double site were in his control and he seemed keen to enter into discussions with us. I confess that from the outset I was apprehensive of dealing in the cut-throat world of London developers, with people who I felt were more than likely to be looking for an angle to rip us off. However, with the reassuring presence of Richard Greeves alongside me, I reasoned that it would be safe to step into the viper's nest.

Dorchester Group put us in touch with their architect, Bruce Calton of Scott Brownrigg. The site was a ramshackle mix of commercial offices and garage unit, used by a photographic studio and a purveyor of corporate branded goods. It was large, being about 50m frontage and about 100m deep. The principal idea was to build a block of residential units across the back where they would have delightful views over the golf course, and a row of townhouses in the middle, all accessed by a private drive down the side. Then our new church centre could be built across the front. It was strange working with an architect who was engaged not by us, but by the developer with whom we were negotiating. Initially he didn't entirely understand our requirements. I had drawn up a draft accommodation schedule, which detailed our wish-list of the number and sizes of rooms and halls. Furnished with that, Bruce soon managed to come up with a plan for what would've been an amazing state-of-the-art church on two floors.

Pic 6.1 Dorchester Group site, High Road between North Finchley and Whetstone.

One issue that needed to be addressed was the fact that not only was this site in the parish of St Johns Whetstone, but it was actually very close to St Johns church itself. Standing in front of the site it is possible to see St Johns diagonally across the road. In my naivety I assumed that this would not be too much of a problem. After all St Johns and St Bs were very different churches; one was a formal high liturgical church with robed clergy, incense and traditional hymns; the other was a contemporary non-liturgical church with worship to a loud band. The people of St Johns would hate to worship at St Bs and vice versa. In other words, I could see little conflict of interest, as we were not in competition with each other. Of course, church leaders always say that they are not in competition with other churches, but where churches are of a similar hue, inevitably there is a tendency to all be fishing in the same pool. However, this was not the case with St Bs and St Johns, so in my mind I thought we should be able to have a complimentary symbiotic relationship. We would be the loud brash young church putting on conferences, courses and youth events. They would be the contemplative formal church, ideal for weddings and funerals. Perhaps we could work together for the benefit of both.

With the proposal on the table, the Archdeacon and I went to visit the PCC[33] of St Johns. By this time, the former curate at St Johns, Cindy Kent was now part-time priest in charge, on a house-for-duty package. Cindy was in effect a volunteer vicar, supplied with the vicarage to live in. Having been a pop star in the 1960s and still one

---

[33] PCC stands for Parochial Church Council, which is a largely elected group that acts as trustees for the church.

of the main anchors on Premier Radio, Cindy was well used to commanding the floor. She had a natural assertive authority and could be quite outspoken, especially on her prime topic: feminism. As an energetic priest her efforts were already yielding results and St Johns was on the up. When I told her about the proposed site, she was understandably apprehensive. Being a neighbour to a church the size of St Barnabas is not an easy thing. Often smaller churches feel embattled and when they see their young people going off and joining the bright lights next door, they feel like they are being robbed of their life. Sitting on the other side of that divide I understand their concern, but also realise that being empathetic shouldn't become a reason to dumb down our mission simply for the sake of our neighbour's sensibilities. The gospel mustn't be constrained by our insecurities. We're not meant to be in competition with each other.

The PCC was meeting in Cindy's lounge in the upstairs vicarage behind the church. I strode confidently in behind the Archdeacon to join the dozen or so council members arrayed around the room. After explaining the plan, I sat back to receive any questions; then the onslaught commenced. I had seriously underestimated the level of unease that St John's PCC was feeling. When I said that we were not in competition and that I wanted to work together with them to both our benefits, the riposte came that I was being disingenuous, as St Bs had a history of proselytizing in their parish. I was shocked and didn't know what to say. Yes of course our people drop leaflets about St Bs activity all over the place, including in other parishes. We have small groups meeting in many parts of the borough of Barnet and beyond. But we live in London, not some isolated village, and people travel widely for work, leisure, friends, clubs and general living. The idea of a fortress mentality, where parish mission work-to-rule on geographic boundaries is completely contradictory to London life. Nevertheless, there was nothing I could say to allay their concerns. I was, to them, the aggressive trespasser, and no doubt they feared that, just as their church was starting to recover under a new inspirational vicar, they were about to be crushed by the invading Goliath from next door. I came out of the meeting feeling pretty mauled. The Archdeacon was sympathetic but had not spoken up for me, no doubt feeling that he had to take a non-partisan line. I went home shattered, knowing that we had little or no chance of progressing on that site; it was simply too much of a political hot potato with our neighbours, for the church authorities to contemplate such a drastic alteration to the parish boundaries. I went to bed that night wondering what would become of it all.

It transpired that there were more problems with the site than the upset with our neighbouring parish PCC. We became aware that, despite Gary Silver's assertions, Dorchester Group had not managed to gain control of both sides of the site. No agreement had been reached and what had looked like a solid prospect, was at a far earlier stage of site compilation[34] than we had thought. There was in effect no viable site available and what with the anxieties of St Johns, it was clearly time to move on.

---

[34] Many years later the site was eventually successfully amalgamated and at the time of writing is fully developed as flats and townhouses on a scheme remarkably similar to the one we had planned all those years ago, only with an extra block of flats at the front where we had envisaged our new church. We were mercifully delivered from interminable delays on this very slow moving development.

It was January 2012 and we reported to our PCC the failure to date of our search for a site for the new church centre. In an emotional report, born of exasperation, I said that I was praying for a site this year; in 2012. The PCC was also frustrated and impatient that this project could not be allowed to drag on interminably. Brian Shearer, a sage-like elder statesman on the PCC, who with his wife Val had been one of the original couples who had joined John Coles in the very early days of the renewal of St Bs, spoke to the hushed gathering: "is it sight or site?" So it was that we resolved that we should make it our objective to either acquire a site in 2012, or at least have sight of a site by the end of the year. This felt like God directing our paths. For me this was always more of a prophetic roadmap than an ultimatum and I relished seeing how God was going to move in our situation. Now we had a time-boundaried goal, and I left the meeting full of faith that at last we were going to see God provide for us.

It wasn't long before another possible site presented itself. The heartache of the failure of the Dorchester Group site nearer St Johns faded in its weight of significance, the bruises of that journey healed; we had moved on. We now expressed serious interest in this new site. This time the developers were a Whetstone company called Turnhold and we were dealing with their CEO Garry Simpson. From the outset Richard Greeves and I felt that Turnhold were the sort of company that we could do business with. They were professional and gave the appearance of wanting to be honest and upfront in their dealings. Discussions were taking place at their rabbit warren of offices, a few doors up from Waitrose on the Whetstone High Road. Turnhold had acquired the old

Furnitureland site, just one block up from Sainsburys on the North Finchley High Road. Furnitureland had been a vast furniture retailer sprawling through the ground floor of a hideous and rather dilapidated 1930s concrete monstrosity, that spanned an entire block between Mayfield Avenue and Friern Watch Avenue. Like with the previous site, it was located in the parish of St Johns, but near the southern most extremity of that parish. Once more we were put in touch with Turnhold's architects: Alan Camp Architects. The site had an enormous frontage onto the High Road but was very shallow. However, whilst restricted, it was still quite large, and we only needed about half the site to comfortably accommodate us. Outline plans were duly drawn up, and although there was still much detail to be worked out, the setting and size of the proposals looked ideal.

Turnhold was interested in proceeding on the basis of a site swap, whereby they would acquire our site in Holden Road in return for the new site on the High road. Garry Simpson seemed a very reasonable man and all was set fair for the project going ahead. Perhaps at last God was going to answer my prayers and we were going to be able to make progress with the relocation project. However, over the summer I noticed that Turnhold had gone rather quiet on us and come September we got the news that Turnhold had been talking to the Housing Association, Catalyst. Housing associations, by providing social and affordable housing, work on a different funding basis than commercial developers. Using government backed funding they are able to pay for sites up front, and it soon became clear that Catalyst were now offering Turnhold (who by this time had changed their name to Landhold)

Pic 6.2 Old Furnitureland site, North Finchley High Road.

an offer they would be foolish to pass up. By the end of the autumn, it was all over for us. The inapplicably named Landhold had agreed to sell out to Catalyst. Britain was in the midst of the post banking crisis austerity, when the market was distinctly wobbly, and the offer of cash in hand was simply too good to refuse.

One year on from the PCC's "site or sight" edict, having spent virtually the entire twelve months negotiating on a potentially excellent site, we were left with nothing to show for our efforts. The whole escapade was going nowhere, and I was becoming desperate. And so it was that in January 2013 I called the church to a week of prayer and fasting.

Chapter 7 –
The moment the Spirit broke through

January 2013 will live long in the memory for all of us at St Bs. It was to be a defining moment in the epic voyage of what was to become known as the "Go and Grow" project. At the time we didn't know what the future journey held for us, but we still had a strong sense that something significant was emerging; that God was on the move.

It was not unusual for us to hold a prayer and fasting season early in the new year, but what was different this time was that we had a specific focus. Years of endless searching for a place to relocate our church had led us time and time again up blind alleys and now we were exhausted, demoralised and perplexed. What was God saying in all this? Were we going in entirely the wrong direction? Should we give up on the idea altogether?

So, we got down on our knees. From Sunday 13th through to Saturday 19th January we ran some twenty meetings where prayer was the focus. As with all prayer vigils there were good times when our hearts were stirred and our spirits invigorated. And there were all the other times, when nothing much seemed to be happening. During this particular week, nothing especially noteworthy seemed to happen until the final meeting.

On the Saturday evening about a hundred of us gathered in the main church. We worshipped and prayed for about one and a half hours. It was a lovely time of worship, one of those times when we could have stayed in that place cherishing God's presence amongst us. But I knew we had an agenda and our spirit kissed worship must inevitably be only a pregnant pause. So, towards the end of the evening, I asked all of us to seek the Lord's voice. We spent a time of quiet waiting on the Lord for Him to speak to us. Then, from that place of being at the very end of our faith reserves, something amazing happened.

The week before the week of prayer and fasting, Richard Greeves, the Chartered Surveyor who was helping us try to find a site, had been driving home from church when he passed a large red brick building on the North Finchley High Road. He stopped and felt God say to him that this was the building He would move the church to. Richard phoned me and pointed me to this High Road building, telling me that he thought it could be converted. I decided I should go and take a look. Somehow, I got the impression that the property was coming on the market and I felt an urgency to check out this prospect. Richard hadn't given me an exact address but had described the property to me. Being only just round the corner from where I live, I wandered down the High Road and quickly identified the property that Richard was referring to. It was a very large 1980s red brick office block. Despite its inherent ugliness and the fact that it was quite unlike a church in almost every respect, my heart started to race. It was a gigantic building, which I must have walked past hundreds of times and yet I had not previously paid any attention to it. But now I looked at it with new eyes; there was something about it that seemed to fulfil so many of the dreams I had had over the past decade and more. Like

Mary storing up things in her heart[35], I walked slowly home wondering what all this could mean.

At the final Saturday night prayer meeting just over a week later, we waited on the Lord for what felt like a long time of quiet. Then out of the silence, one-by-one people began to give "words" they felt God was saying to us: "the church is going to be like a beacon in North Finchley", "we're going to be a blazing fire on the High Road and it is about the building", "we are going to be light that all can see", "we're going to be a star shining in the darkness" and finally from Isaiah 60:1 'Arise, shine, for your light has come, and the glory of the LORD rises upon you'.[36]

The building Richard had pointed me to was called "Solar House".

Pic 7.1 Solar House.

It turned out that I had been completely mistaken in thinking that it was about to come on the market and for

---

[35] Luke 2:19.
[36] We have since had this verse etched into our glass entrance doors.

just that one week, the week of prayer and fasting, I was under this misapprehension. The property was not due to come on the market, it was just another property on the High Road, owned by someone else, who was blissfully unaware of our existence, let alone our interest.

Little did we know then what a tempestuous voyage we were embarking on. But back then, freshly envisioned by the voice of God, we set off boldly to realise the dream that God had placed before us. Over the next year, we did three things which, but for the words of God given to us, would be viewed as, at best eccentric, and at worst barking mad.

Appointing an Architect

First, we decided we should start by appointing our own architect. We needed to find out whether this property was indeed convertible to a church. Office blocks are not the most natural candidate for church conversions, and generally buildings that have been repurposed as churches have cavernous interiors like old cinemas or warehouses. So, we decided to run what is euphemistically called a "beauty contest". We invited a selection of architects to submit feasibility studies on the conversion of Solar House to a church. In doing so we were killing two birds with one stone; we would get the answers to our questions on the feasibility of the project, and we would also appoint our architect.

So, feeling slightly like some elaborate hoaxer, we sent our briefing papers for a feasibility study on a building that we didn't own, wasn't in our parish, wasn't on the market and for which we had no money. We had just one advocate for the veracity of our case; the Holy Spirit.

In the event, just two of the circulated architects chose to submit proposals. Such studies take a lot of work and so professional architectural firms have to be quite circumspect about which client prospects to invest a lot of staff time into, without any guarantee of a return. In our case it was interesting that both the architects that threw their hats into the ring were Christian church-specialist practices. The more commercial and general based practices probably took one look at the project and concluded that it was completely bonkers. Sometimes it takes the eyes of faith to see beyond the objections.

We set a date for the architects to visit us, with the first company doing their presentation in the morning and the other one in the afternoon. At some point in the years of deliberating over our future building needs, we had gone to the trouble of drawing up a refined wish list. Based on our vision and the guiding principles of the project, we set four main attributes that we wanted in our new church centre.

The desired four main attributes were:

a) **High profile location**. For the sake of mission, we wanted to be in the heart of the community, rather than stuck in an invisible back road. We also had a vision to become a large regional hub church, and to do that we would need to be in place that is not only easy to get to, but a well-known highly visible centre. Fortunately, Solar House was in such a location.

b) **A large centre**. Based on the accommodation schedule that we had drawn up all those years before we knew that we needed between 24,000 and 30,000 sq ft of floor space in the building to accommodate all our ministries and room for growth. Only about ¼ of this would be used as the main auditorium. With an internal usable floor area of 36,500 sq ft, plus stair wells and lobbies, we knew that Solar house had sufficient space for our needs.

c)   **A purpose-built building**. A brand-new purpose-built church centre would be far more efficient than a converted old building. This was one of the reasons we had rejected the conversion of the old St Barnabas building, as what we were intending was a long way from what our forebears envisaged when they built St Barnabas nearly 100 years ago. But now we were looking at the possible conversion of a building arguably far more unsuitable for conversion to a modern church centre than our old building. Overcoming the problems involved in repurposing an existing building was undoubtedly the biggest challenge we were looking to our architect to resolve.

d)   **A landmark building**. Whilst we believe that buildings are essentially only tools, they can also be inspiring. We wanted a building, and in particular a main worship space, that would be evocative and inspirational. This was by no means an easy fix in a building like Solar House.

The day of the beauty contest arrived. The morning architect presented some ambiguous plans that confirmed what, in my darker moments, I had been thinking. The property was not really suitable for conversion. The big problem was how to create an inspiring worship space. With low ceilings clad in office style ceiling tiles, the whole place looked and felt like an office. Putting the main sanctuary on the top floor[37], where there might be the opportunity to create an elevated ceiling, was quickly ruled out for the sheer difficulty of moving that number of people up to a third floor. There was very limited space round the back to build on, so options seemed to have run out. By lunchtime I was starting to feel a bit discouraged. Where was this leading? We had spent the morning with one of the best-respected architects in the field and yet none of the answers were positive.

The afternoon could not have been more different. The cheerful, charismatic architect, Kelvin Samson, in a single stroke of genius swept away the intractable design problems. He proposed knocking down a small three storey spur on the back of the building. The result was to create a huge space out the back of the property on which to build a purpose built 500 seat sanctuary. Not only had Kelvin managed to find a way of enabling the building of an inspiring main auditorium, but he had also managed to make at least part of the building purpose-built, thereby negating some of the negative aspects of a converted building. Kelvin worked in a practice called JBKS, named after the initials of its two founding partners, Jeremy Bell and Kelvin Sampson. They were based in Oxfordshire but working with churches all over the country. We went on to appoint them as our architects for the project, but it would be Kelvin's partner Jeremy Bell who was to end up as our lead architect, while Kelvin was later to move on.

---

[37] Amazingly Emmanuel Church, Brighton (formerly known as "Christ the King"), has done just that. When they converted an old Comet warehouse, they added an extra floor to create an 800 seat auditorium on the top floor. I still can't quite work out how they get everyone up there, but it seems to work fine.

Applying to move the parish boundaries

Unlike our first sortie into attempting to find a High Road development site, Solar House was only just outside our parish. In fact, only the road Fredericks Place came between us and this new territory. Nevertheless, the site was still outside our parish and in the parish of St Johns Whetstone. Matters concerning parish boundaries are governed by the Church Commissioners, a centralised institution that is responsible for the high-level running of the Church of England. In practice, the organisation is run by the church's equivalent of civil servants and much of its business goes on quietly behind closed doors in Church House in Westminster. Getting through to the Church Commissioners is not easily achieved, and for this, we needed the contacts of our friends at the diocese.

Over the years I have had many dealings with the property department of the diocese. They would've been forgiven had they stopped taking me seriously after such a long time of hopeless trails. However, in Michael Bye, the diocesan head of property, we had always found someone whom you intuitively sensed was on your side. Michael, a chirpy Chartered Surveyor with a sharp eye for an opportunity, is a likeable, friendly man, whose affability belies his tough and tenacious interior. Once we had identified Solar House as the property we wanted to try to acquire, we immediately got onto the diocese, and specifically Michael, to see what to do next. We had been round this block before, but somehow it seemed more serious this time. One of the things Michael did for us was to put us in touch with the Church Commissioners.

Our case was to be handled by Church Commissioners' mandarin Harvey Howlett, a slightly Dickensian gentleman with a penchant for bright waistcoats. I had met Harvey years before and found him to be sympathetic to our cause. This had not been what I had initially expected, as everything about him seemed to suggest someone who would be deeply conservative. The idea of this man partnering with a radical vicar, with a plan to trade in his Edwardian church for an eighties office block, seemed improbable to say the least. However, most of Harvey's work involved closing down churches whose congregations had dwindled to the point of near extinction. In comparison to this dispiriting work, the opportunity to help facilitate a story of life and growth was perhaps gladdening to him, as he was ever encouraging and cheerful with us.

Moving a parish boundary is a complex legal process. Various notices are required to be posted, people consulted, and any representations heard. With Harvey attending to the legal requirements, I was asked to go and once more consult St Johns Whetstone. Having been at the receiving end of fairly rough treatment from St John's PCC, I was not keen to go back for a second round. However, I got on well with their vicar Revd Cindy Kent and hoped it would be sufficient to meet with her and the Churchwardens, Brian Wakeham and Rob Wright. Early in September 2013 I set off for the St John's vicarage with a knot in my stomach. Cindy cut through the small talk: "Where is it this time?" I got out a parish map and pointed to the Solar House site on the extreme edge of their parish, adjacent to the boundary with ours. Then, looking at my pointing figure, before either of the wardens could speak, Cindy declared: "Oh, that's fine". They were clearly relieved, that having had the prospect of us as unwanted neighbours on their doorstep, we were now proposing being half a mile down the road. Yes, they would be giving us a small portion of their geographic parish, but I think they immediately realised that there would be zero effect on their church.

As a result of that meeting, the alteration to the parish boundaries went ahead unopposed. I am grateful to St Johns for not raising an objection, that would have inevitably mired us in endless rounds of officialdom and thereby possibly sunk the entire project. There were still a lot of hoops to jump through, but with the good offices of Harvey Howlett to navigate us, we felt confident that this would be achieved.

Setting up structure and finance for the project

The moment God identified Solar House to us in that auspicious prayer meeting back in January 2013, I knew it would take a miracle to achieve the dream. However, God's purposes will not be thwarted and somehow, we had faith that a way through would be found. To acquire Solar House was going to take lots of money and we had none. Eventually we planned to sell off our existing church, probably for development, and that would provide a certain amount of funds, but that would be years down the road. We had a cash flow problem, we needed money, a lot of money.

St Barnabas is a large church, but not a rich church. From the outside people look at our accounts and see the hundreds of thousands of pounds that it takes to run this vibrant community and conclude that we must be rolling in it. This is far from the truth. Most of the time St Bs lives by faith, with just enough money coming in to cover our immediate expenses. So, to find millions of pounds for a speculative venture would be completely beyond us. I thought about the wealthy people who I knew, yet none of them were in this kind of league, even if they had been willing. And then I thought about the diocese. The diocese was wealthy, it had huge reserves; could they be persuaded to lend me some of their funds to kick-start the project? So, we pitched for a loan from the diocese of up to £9million. It was probably a good thing that I didn't know that this was many times more than what the diocese had ever loaned to a single project before.

The diocese's general secretary, the equivalent of the CEO of the business aspect of the diocese, was Andy Brookes. Andy was a tall, bicycle riding, visionary leader, who exuded smiling confidence that one sometimes encounters in very senior executives. Andy had a lively faith and attended a North London evangelical parish not far from us. When we met with him, he told us that he was keen to leverage the diocesan balance sheet for mission, and whilst I knew he was no pushover, I sensed that we had a potential ally. It was providential that we just happened to make our approach for funds to the diocese during the relative short tenure of Andy Brookes. It was perhaps, this never to be repeated window, when Andy's entrepreneurial outlook momentarily caused the famously cautious diocese to be more adventurous, that made a positive outcome possible. Of course, I do not believe that such fortuity was luck; clearly the invisible hand of God was guiding events.

In order for us to borrow the vast sums we would need from the diocese, there needed to be a robust governance structure and legal framework. Over the course of months, we agreed a joint project board with three members from the diocese and three members from St Bs.

The board was to operate under the aegis of a "relationship agreement", in which we detailed out how decisions were to be taken and what would happen if we were in dispute. In the event of the board being unable to agree on an issue, it would be taken to the Bishop of London for arbitration and his decision would be final and binding. Within the relationship agreement a so called "parenting clause" was included. This gave the diocesan side of the project board the right to pull the plug on the project should they deem, in their role as our parent, that their child (St Barnabas) was being irresponsible. This, like everything else, was subject to appeal to the Bishop of London. From our side, we were hesitant about the clause, but the diocese insisted, and we had little choice but to go along with it. Later the clause was invoked and proved controversial, but on balance I can admit in hindsight that it was a good thing it was there.

The membership of the project board comprised on our side: me, Richard Greeves, and Hannah Parker, an accountant who was also on our PCC. From the diocesan side it was: Andy Brookes, the Archdeacon of Hampstead: The Ven. Luke Miller, and another property professional called Andrew Garwood Watkins. The Archdeacon was to be the chair.

Pic 7.2 Hannah Parker, Richard Greeves and me.

With this structure in place, a request for the loan was to be put to the diocesan finance committee and to the diocesan trustees. I sit on several charity trust boards and thought I knew the form. Generally, a charity board will have a chair, a treasurer, a secretary (who does much of the work), one or two people knowledgeable in the field and an executive who has his or her feet on the ground. So, most boards are six or seven strong. When I looked up the diocesan trustees, I was astonished to find that they numbered fifty-six. Most of them were senior clergy of a very different churchmanship to us, who had spent much of their lives trying to retain the fine old traditions of the Church of England. As an up-and-coming church, espousing contemporary worship, I doubted we would find much support for our cause. In my imagination I saw a room full of dusty clerics who hated everything we stood for. Fifty-six of them.

As the day of the trustees' decision approached, I sent round urgent prayer requests to our intercessors. Surely it was hopeless; the diocese had never lent such an immense amount to anyone before, let alone for such a radical proposal. Yet we had no alternative plan; if this loan request failed, we would be back once more at square one, wondering where God was leading us.

The Diocesan finance committee met on Thursday 13th February 2014 and amazingly agreed to our loan proposal. Now it just had to be ratified by the trustees who were due to meet a couple of weeks later. It had been just over a year since we started on the mission to acquire Solar House at the culmination of the week of prayer and fasting, but now virtually everything was in place. If the trustees agreed, all we would need was for the owners of Solar House to be willing to sell.

Jane and I were seizing the opportunity afforded by half term to celebrate our thirtieth wedding anniversary with a city break to Madrid. Whilst my mind was racing on matters concerning the project, I was determined to go and have a good time. We disembarked at the airport and got on a bus to take us into central Madrid. Whilst on the bus, to my great surprise my mobile rang: it was Richard. He had astonishing news: out of the blue, Solar House was coming onto the market. That phone call was one of those moments when life changes in a split second, I felt a physical surge of adrenalin as I heard the news. I turned to Jane and said "If this deal flies it will change my life for the next five years." This was God's doing and nothing was going to stop us now.

SOLAR HOUSE
915 HIGH ROAD, FINCHLEY N12 8QJ
Multilet Office Building with Development Opportunity
LEWIS ☻ PARTNERS

Pic 7.3 Lewis and Partners' Solar House Brochure.

The owners of Solar House were expecting to sell it for redevelopment as flats under permitted development rights (PDR)[38] and with this element of the market booming, were asking for offers within just two weeks. We had to wait another five days before the diocesan trustees met. Staggeringly, despite all my fears, the fifty-six dusty cleric trustees duly ratified the finance committee's recommendation. I would have loved to be a fly on the wall in that trustees meeting. What were they thinking? Did they know what they had just agreed to? I imagined it was a bit like the sleeping old man twitching at the wrong moment in an auction, only to find that he had purchased a property. I wondered what this group of trustees thought later when the project languished. But at that moment, at the end of February 2014, the diocesan trustees marvellously blinked in the light of the Holy Spirit's glare. And so, through what I consider a series of miraculous occurrences, after a year of making arrangements, with perfect timing, we found ourselves in a position to make an offer within the vendor's two-week window.

---

[38] Permitted development rights are a special measure by the government to allow the conversion of office blocks into residential flats without the need for planning permission. Whilst certain permissions do need to be obtained, these are much cheaper than applying for full planning consent. Hence office blocks that are potentially eligible for PDR become very saleable.

Chapter 8
Purchase complexities

The owners of Solar House, a property investment company called Topland, had judged the market perfectly. Dozens of eager developers lined up to put in their bids. They had set the asking price at a relatively modest level, and so we decided to make a bid close to that. It was immediately turned down and we quickly convened an emergency meeting of our PCC; the first of many. Having been lulled into a false optimism by the relatively low asking price, the offer rejection served as a cold glass of water thrown into our face to wake us up to the harsh realities of the real world. The PCC courageously agreed to a substantially increased bid. After the inevitable jostling for position, we had made the very best bid we could afford and were told that we were among the frontrunners.

Pic 8.1 Me submitting our offer on Richard Greeves' ipad in the middle of a prayer meeting.

Then the news came that we had been significantly outbid and that Topland had agreed a sale to the developer that had made the top offer. I was stunned. I had been so certain that this had been God's provision. Head in hands I sat in utter dejection. How was I going to tell the church that all our plans lay in tatters? Where was God's provision? Everything we had worked for over the last year, with every piece of the jigsaw falling into place, was blown to smithereens. It didn't make sense.

In the midst of our despair and confusion, David Brown, our discipleship pastor and one of the wisest people I know, shared a scripture: "We do not know what to do, but our eyes are on you." (2 Chronicles 20:12) That one verse said everything. I had no other answer, so I clung to that verse. We prayed and we worshipped, and we kept our eyes on God. We didn't understand, but we knew we had to trust.

> "We do not know what to do, but our eyes are on you."
> (2 Chronicles 20:12)

Life continued as normal, but I felt like a zombie vicar. I wandered around in a fog of unreality, puzzling over why God had led us so clearly, only to see our goal snatched away at the final moment. Where had we gone so wrong? Had we been disobedient to the voice of God? I knew we hadn't. I believe in a benevolent God who loves us as our father, but this episode looked more like a cruel parent who shows a child a sweet only to snatch it away. Jesus taught us to ask, seek, knock and be assured of a positive answer[39]. Jesus, speaking on the loving provision of Father-God, went on to say "Which of you fathers, if your son asks for a fish, will give him a snake instead? Or if he

---

[39] Luke 11:9-10.

asks for an egg, will give him a scorpion?" [40] Yet it looked to me like I had been given a snake or a scorpion.

For a few weeks I placed one foot in front of the other on a blind walk of faith, not knowing what lay ahead. Then, as quickly as the gloom had descended, it evaporated. The high bidder had inexplicably pulled out. Topland were back talking to us, checking us out, negotiating details. The deal was on! Incredibly, against all the odds, with a pack of developers snapping at our heels, the vendors of Solar House had agreed to sell the property to us.

Strictly speaking, of course, the sale was not to us, St Bs, but to the diocese. The relationship agreement that we had with the diocese specified the level of risk that we had to bear, and the limit to that. In the event of the deal going bad and us making huge losses, we were exposed to the point of being committed to reimburse the diocese the first £1.1million of any shortfall. Beyond that, the diocese would shoulder the loss. I looked at this and didn't lose any sleep. God had directed us to purchase this property and so God would provide a way ahead. In any case, it was a valuable property, and the market was rising, so even if everything went wrong and we had to sell out, the chances were that we would come out with a profit, not a loss. However, my friends at the diocese did not share my optimism. Despite the fact that we at St Bs would pay for any initial losses and that the diocese would only lose money if the overall loss exceeded £1.1m, there was extreme nervousness around Diocesan House. Much of our energies over the next few years were to be focused on keeping our lenders (the diocese) calm.

---

[40] Luke 11:11-12.

Right from the outset the priority for the diocese was to have a viable exit strategy. So pressing was this concern that, much to my frustration, more time was spent planning and providing for the exit strategy than for the going ahead strategy. With such competition from other purchasers, we were proposing to buy Solar House straight away without any planning permissions. In order to protect the diocese's investment, we decided that we needed to apply for permission under PDR (permitted development rights[41]) to convert the building into residential flats. So, bizarrely, an architect was commissioned, plans were drawn up and consultations were made, all about a plan that we had no intention of seeing come to fruition. "So you're planning to convert it into flats." I was asked. "No," I stuttered in reply, "it's complicated." Once we had the PDR permissions in place the property would be 'oven-ready' for development and therefore easily and quickly re-saleable. This was the best way of guaranteeing that the diocese would be able to recover their money in the event of the project collapsing.

Pic 8.2 Me pretending to look confident outside Solar House for the Barnet Times Newspaper in 2014.

---

[41] See chapter 7.

Apart from our own internal arrangements for safeguarding the diocese's money, the negotiations to purchase Solar House from Topland were inordinately complex. There was more than one buyer: the diocese as the initial buyer, but St Bs being the real buyer behind the scenes. There were tenants in the property to consider. There was the allied sale of our existing church in Holden Road. But far and away the most difficult issue to address was that of VAT.

No one in the treasury legislature would set out to create a tax that hard-bitten, commercial companies wouldn't have to pay and charities would, but that is the end result with VAT. The relevance of this to us was that commercial property is liable to VAT. If we had been a business, trading for a profit, this would not have been a problem, as we would simply claim the VAT back, or not pay in the first place under an exemption[42]. But as a charity the VAT would, if we were not careful, end up being fully chargeable. This was no small matter as, with VAT charged at 20%, we might have ended up with a tax bill of about £1½ million. Such an additional cost would make the entire project inviable, and we would've had to immediately abort. There are lots of exemptions in order to mitigate some of VAT's problems, but all of these have complexities, and we would have to be very careful to pick our way through the web of trip hazards if we were to avoid catastrophe.

---

[42] The most common exemption to paying VAT on a commercial property purchase is TOGC: Transfer of a Going Concern. This roughly means that where a company can show that their property purchase is an ongoing part of their business, they become exempt from paying the VAT on it.

We decided to retain tax specialist Deliottes to advise us. At this point I entered an entirely different world. Vicars rarely mix with other professionals in the course of their work. The nearest we come to it is dealing with undertakers while making funeral arrangements. But whilst they are invariably professional in the way they conduct themselves, their world of parochial burials is a long way from the high-powered throbbing heart of the city of London's financiers. We went to meet the VAT tax partner at Deliottes, Kevin White, with his sidekick David Tennet. As Deliotte's top man on the subject, Kevin's time was charged at £1000 per hour (plus VAT), and no doubt we were also paying for the sidekick to be there. Kevin, a large jovial man, vaguely reminiscent in my mind of Shakespeare's Falstaff, started by exchanging pleasantries, but all I could think of was the clock ticking and the money burning. The meeting actually went very well and Kevin was confident that we could legitimately avoid paying VAT, but had to put certain things in place first.

Solar House had a large frontage onto the High Road with a single main entrance off-centre. Either side of this entrance are the two wings of the property, divided roughly one-third and two-thirds. Since our original feasibility study, we had refined the plans and now accepted that we only needed the larger two-thirds South Wing to fulfil our accommodation needs. Under our VAT strategy we needed the South Wing, which we intended to occupy, to be vacant at the point of purchase. However, at the time there were still tenants on the South Wing's ground and third floors. The tenants on the third floor, an events company called Aspect, had recently trimmed down their operations and didn't need so much space.

They were keen to move from the South Wing to the North Wing where the floor area and the rent were about half, which conveniently freed up the space that we needed to be vacant on the third floor. The ground floor was more difficult. The Tenants were a serviced office company called Brentano and they currently occupied both wings of the ground floor of the building. There was no obvious solution as this was a successful growing company and they wanted the space. The negotiations were complicated by the fact that Brentano's contractual relationship was with the current owners Topland, not with us. So, discussions had to be conducted vicariously through Topland. Eventually, after quite protracted negotiations, we persuaded them to move out of the ground floor of the South Wing into the second floor of the North Wing and agreed a compensation package for them.

Meanwhile, in the background we were working hard on a prudent budget for the project. It was fast becoming abundantly clear that the overall cost of the project would be higher than we had imagined. The implications of this were that we would have to sell more assets, raise more money, if possible get a large mortgage, and plan to sell off the North Wing. We had hoped to keep the North Wing as an investment that gave us overall control of the entire building. It would also give us the potential opportunity to grow into the space if needed and so the whole project would be generously future-proofed. But we couldn't make the numbers work whilst the North Wing was kept in our ownership. So, with great reluctance we had to acknowledge that we could not afford to keep the North Wing and that we should plan to sell it.

Part of the plan to fund the project was to hold the upper floors of Solar House in a separate hereditament that would be available as a mortgageable asset. Various enquiries were made about us taking a mortgage. However, for a mortgagee to agree a loan, they would not only want to see sufficient value as collateral, but would also want to be assured that there is an adequate revenue stream available to pay the ongoing monthly interest and repayments. Our annual accounts over the last few years amply demonstrated that we had been able to meet our existing liabilities, but no more than that. At St Bs our finances have always been a hand to mouth existence. This is not just a fiscal reality for us, but a theological position. Jesus instructed his disciples to take no purse for the journey.[43] In other words, we have never seen protecting our backs by running a surplus as something desirable. Faith is a fragile thing and risk-aversion and nest-egg cooping tend to move our hearts towards self-reliance, rather than a radical trust in God. So, we have always preferred to live life 'on the way,' spending what God provides. Now, facing bankers, the edgy state of our finances was counting against us.

With no obvious way of changing the banks minds, it became clear that it would not be possible to achieve the entire project in one go. We decided that for the project to be able to go ahead we would need to realise it in two phases. The first phase would be the conversion of the existing building from an office block to a church centre, with a new entrance, new toilets, new kitchens, new stairs and lift, and new room layouts. The second phase would be the demolition of the three-storey spur on the back of

---

[43] Matthew 10:9.

the building and the construction of the new church sanctuary, a superb 500-seat auditorium. However, in order to maintain the ministry of the church throughout, we would also need to plan for the period of construction of the auditorium, when we would already be in occupation of the building. Elaborate plans were detailed to accommodate all the church's activities in different spaces, while the majority of the ground floor became a building site. We dubbed this project-stage "the camping phase".

As 2014 moved on, we were coming under increasing pressure from the vendors Topland to exchange contracts. In fact, they had been incredibly patient with us, especially bearing in mind that a list of alternative buyers, who doubtless had none of the complex encumbrances that we laboured under, waited in the wings. Deadlines to exchange of contracts came and went, and still they persevered with us.

Chapter 9
The launch of Go and Grow

By the time we publicly launched the "Go and Grow" project at St Barnabas, in September 2014, we had already been working flat out behind the scenes for more than eighteen months. We planned an eight-week campaign to inform and inspire the church, culminating in receiving pledges for giving to the project. We needed to raise a fortune.

The launch was an invigorating, if exhausting, experience. By the end of that Sunday, I had spoken multiple times and received numerous words of encouragement and support at the end of the services. St Barnabas is an amazing church to be part of, and I felt my own conviction rising as I saw the groundswell of faith in the St Bs community start to rise inexorably, like a river in flood about to burst its banks. Preaching on Moses that day made me realise how often we rely on human adequacy, either in ourselves or in others we are trusting. The magnitude of the Go and Grow project for St Bs had brought this into sharp relief, because depending on our resources and abilities was simply not an option. The challenge was so great it was obvious to anyone that this would be way beyond us. If St Barnabas were, to any extent, to depend on my abilities, we would be destined for a big let-down. I am simply inadequate; not up to the task.

During a particularly difficult day working on the Go and Grow project I sometimes found myself giving in to feelings of being utterly overwhelmed. All my insecurities rose to the surface and in the face of such enormous responsibility, I would often get cowed by the burden. However, there is a different option; an alternative way to react to this overpowering situation - by looking to God to supply all our needs. To follow this route of faith needs to be a positive decision. I decided to take the faith route, to trust God and not myself and all of a sudden, things that previously were preposterous looked possible again.

This venture had always been a walk of faith and no more so than it was now. It was necessary for us to push full steam ahead before we had certainty on a number of issues. So, we were stepping out and committing ourselves financially and legally, while knowing that there was still a significant risk that the whole project would come crashing down like the proverbial house of cards. Even the upbeat launch of Go and Grow was a step of faith, as we had not yet exchanged contracts on the purchase of Solar House.

The week before, at one meeting with the Archdeacon (I had more than one with him!), he read Psalm 127: 1-2: "Unless the Lord builds the house, the builders labour in vain. Unless the Lord watches over the city, the guards stand watch in vain. In vain you rise early and stay up late, toiling for food to eat – for he grants sleep to those he loves." Perhaps this might be considered to be an obvious text to cite in the circumstances, but it hit me with fresh force. The last season had involved quite a bit of "toiling" for me, Hannah Parker and Richard Greeves[44], and it was a salutary reminder that all our efforts are without consequence unless it is God working through us. However, it was the end of verse 2 that particularly struck me: "The Lord grants sleep to those he loves." This is a verse that I know and love and have often quoted but, for some reason, I had completely forgotten that it comes in the context of the Lord building the house. Sometimes when we are facing huge, stressful and intractable problems we go to bed with our minds still racing. Worrying seems to be becoming practically a national pastime. How different is the walk of faith, where we know that not everything depends on us and that we serve someone who is going to fulfil His plans with or without us. Of course, we are called to play our part, but if we trust in our wonderful benevolent Father God, we are able to rest easy in the sure knowledge that everything will be all right. That is why Jesus, in the midst of a furious storm to the consternation of the disciples, was in the stern of the boat sleeping on a cushion[45]. That night, in faith, I hoped to sleep well.

During the Go and Grow eight-week fundraising push, I spent a day at my publishers (I had written a book that was due for publication the following year) on a resourcing day for authors. Quite a bit of the day was about building a personal platform on social media. I was so glad that I'd started writing a blog because without it I would have felt far behind my fellow authors. Even so, I couldn't get out of my head a nagging thought that I shouldn't even have been there. I confess that my mind

---

[44] The three project board members for St Bs.
[45] Mark 4:38.

had not principally been on my book in recent times, as the Go and Grow project had been gathering pace. Being forced mentally to get back into the world of book publishing made me realise that there is a blatant connection that had not previously occurred to me. My book[46] was about the life of the Spirit - how we can live the life of faith every day. The Go and Grow journey had been, even up to that undeveloped point, the most potent example of doing exactly that. We had pursued what we believed to be God's purposes even when, at times, the whole thing looked crazy. We had seen God move with extraordinary interventions, that could not be reasonably explained by human logic. We had felt as if we were walking on the water, and each time we looked around and saw the wind and waves, we had cried out "Lord save me". We had experienced the faithfulness of God somehow turning every situation around, as if Jesus had reached out his hand and caught us saying, "You of little faith, why did you doubt?"[47] My book may still have been 9 months away from publication, but we were living it in the present.

The launch of the Go and Grow project was principally an exercise of vision casting. We, the small group at the heart of the St Bs leadership, had a vision for relocating our church centre up to new premises on the High Road. But this was of no consequence unless others caught that vision and would travel with us. The way I shaped the vision for the project was through the idea of the five dimensions of Go and Grow.

---

[46] The Wind Blows Wherever it Pleases. Authentic 2015.
[47] Matthew 14:31.

Pic 9.1 Five dimensions

Five dimensions, Five-Fold Impact

St Barnabas' relocation to Solar House on the North Finchley High Road will have a five-fold impact on the church, the communities we serve and the wider church in North London.

1. Community hub

Church should be a place of welcome, an open door, somewhere anyone can feel at home. That's exactly what we plan to create by transforming Solar House into a community hub - a visible building, open to all, where anyone who comes through our door will find a warm welcome, a warm smile and a warm mug of Fairtrade coffee awaiting them.

2. Mission port

Whether through missional communities, long-term overseas partners or short-term teams, St Bs has a strong culture of mission. Far from being a place to put our feet up and retreat inwards, the move to Solar House will give us an even greater springboard for mission - both into our local area, across North London and around the world.

3. Social enterprise

In many quiet ways, we have a track record of helping people turn their lives around - from supporting the long-term unemployed to find their way back into work, to mentoring young people from disadvantaged backgrounds, standing alongside those wrestling free from substance abuse and walking with people through all manner of other fresh starts.

Part of our Go and Grow vision is to supercharge that life-transforming activity by working with entrepreneurs and investors to create new social enterprises that will enable us to provide much more structured opportunities to help many more people.

4. Resourcing Centre

We want to see people equipped to make a difference in their street, school, home and workplace. St Bs already provides many training, mentoring and discipleship opportunities and has repeatedly sent out talented leaders to support other churches near and far.

Through the Go and Grow project, we will transform Solar House into a resourcing centre, increasing our capacity to train, raise up and release individuals to be good news in their neighbourhoods, North London and the nations.

5. Church Base

Having welcomed in the community, fostered local and global mission, supported people in turning their lives around, and invested in the discipling and development of believers across North London, last but not least, through Go and Grow we will create an inspiring church base where our existing members and the many new people who experience the love of Christ through us in the coming years will be able to join together in worship, teaching and community.

There will be better space and more suitable facilities for our Sunday services and all our activities during the week - for kids work, youth work, young adults, families and the elderly. With a more obvious presence on the High Road, we will be able to play a more visible role in the spiritual lives of the people of North Finchley - for weddings, baptisms, christenings and funerals, as well as our major festivals of Christmas and Easter, which we anticipate will attract many more people as a result of our relocation.

During the campaign there came the point when I had to challenge St Bs to sacrifice. Why? Well, firstly you can't become more like Jesus without sacrifice and that is always our principal goal – transformed lives, starting with us. We want to lead people to become more like Jesus. God is a lavishly generous God. Generosity is the flip side of love: "For God so loved the world that he gave".[48] Jesus was the most generous man who ever lived and we can't hope to begin to follow him without learning to be generous. But if becoming more like Jesus was and is our first objective, providing for the future of St Bs was the second. I believed that we would be investing in the greatest cause on earth – the church. As Bill Hybels put it "The local church is the hope of the world". We are the beachhead for the kingdom of God, invading the dominion of darkness with the gospel of Jesus Christ. Of course, buildings don't change the world, but what goes on in them does. We believed that now was the time, a Kairos[49] moment in the life of our church, when God was calling us to step out at a level of faith we had never previously experienced. It would be challenging, scary and very costly.

The autumn of 2014 had been quite a gruelling ordeal for me. In the middle of the Go and Grow fundraising campaign our beloved dog Sam died, and the following day I went to St Bs with a heavy heart, knowing I had to share something very private. This was a crucial moment in the life of St Bs and I had to take a lead. Jane and I had agreed that I should share with the church what we personally would be donating to the Go and Grow project. I have rarely felt so exposed. It felt like being naked before everyone (or rather what I imagine it would feel like to be naked, as I have no idea what that would actually be like) - very uncomfortable. To my surprise, it was received very well. I was very aware that many people have grown up with the perspective that all giving should be in secret.

---

[48] John 3:16a.

[49] Ancient Greek has two words for 'time': Kairos (καιρός) and Chronos (χρόνος). While Chronos means the chronological time, Kairos refers to a critical moment.

And indeed, with regard to giving to those in need, Jesus says that we should "be careful not to practise our righteousness in front of others to be seen by them",[50] and two verses later: "Do not let your left hand know what your right hand is doing."[51] He was of course using hyperbole to make his point, but we would be wise to note that we should never give money, or in any other way, in order to receive plaudits from those around us. If we do, we have had all the reward that we shall ever get. But a special reward of intimacy with God is reserved for those whose hearts are set on pleasing God alone, and don't give a toss what anyone else thinks. So where does all this leave us with regard to secret giving, when the rest of the Bible teaches in numerous places that we should encourage one another, by good example, to be generous. The key surely is the attitude of our hearts. If we're looking to be proud of what we give, then that is our reward. However, if we are seeking to please God, then our treasure is in heaven.

Our Go and Grow project was so large it was frightening. I was aware that when I announced the fund target of £3½ million, it seemed like a fanciful amount. However, other churches have done very large projects before. Our fund target only represented 4¼ times our annual giving income at the time (only!). A number of other churches I had researched had given 8 times their annual income and more. So, I was convinced that it was achievable if we could together catch the vision that God had set before us. The challenge ahead of us was

---

[50] Matthew 6:1.
[51] Matthew 6:3.

considerable, but the potential outcomes could be astonishing.

Over the course of the campaign, we presented the project in various ways. Looking at some of the architects' plans made the project come alive as we started to envisage what the church might feel like in this new building. After an amazing and inspiring evening with our architect Jeremy Bell, we poured over the plans that he had presented. So much of what we had dreamt of for years was now emerging in room-layouts before our eyes. As with all building projects there are of course priorities for some aspects, which inevitably mean compromises for others. But what was becoming clear was that in Solar House we would have better facilities than anything we had previously dared to hope for. Chatting to Jeremy before the meeting I was arrested when he commented that, "St Barnabas is a miracle of what God can do through a church even when it has the most inadequate facilities." It made me realise that living day-in and day-out in our old Edwardian premises had meant that we had no longer been able to see clearly the full perspective of what we had been dealing with. And it was a miracle. God had truly provided for us, enabling St Bs to flourish in really quite difficult circumstances. But the future beckoned. It was uncertain, immensely challenging and very scary. There were still a lot of issues to be overcome. Yet more and more I sensed God on the move.

I was told about one of our longstanding and respected church members at St Bs who had a vision 15 years ago but didn't tell anyone. Then when I was describing the large underground car park at Solar House, her old vision came to mind. What she had seen was St Bs moved into a new building and the building had a large underground car park. It seemed so ridiculous at the time that she simply put it to the back of her mind. But now, 15 years later, she realised that her vision had special relevance. As I heard this, I thought back 15 years to the very first time we had started seriously looking into the prospect of St Bs moving. Unbeknown to her, or to us, a decade and a half earlier God had been speaking simultaneously to both of us.

The move to Solar House on the High Road was becoming a long arduous journey. It was almost as if St Bs had been pregnant for 15 years. The longest gestation in the animal kingdom is the African Elephant at just under 2 years, so by any measure 15 years is a long time. Although the waiting had tested my patience to breaking point, I found it reassuring to know that God had known every detail of this project all along, from timings to car parks. The journey was far from complete, and many mountains and valleys lay ahead, with significant risks of the whole thing collapsing. Yet God knows the end from the beginning and is utterly trustworthy.

I was talking to someone before a Sunday service at St Bs about the move to the High Road. She said, "It's not about the building, it's about God's presence". I was immediately reminded of the incident in Exodus 33 when Moses was anxiously talking to God "Then Moses said to him, 'If your Presence does not go with us, do not send us up from here. How will anyone know that you are pleased with me and with your people unless you go with us? What else will distinguish me and your people from all the other people on the face of the earth?'[52] The one characteristic we craved was not to be known for fine

---

[52] Exodus 33

buildings, with or without stone arches, but to be a people of God's presence. It should be a distinctive of our church community that others comment on and wonder about. This is not something that can be worked up or contrived. It is borne out of a faith community seeking the face of God above all else, and as a result, knowing God speaking to them and manifesting his glory among them. Paul once said that if unbelievers see a truly prophetic church they will fall down and worship God, exclaiming, "God is really among you!"[53] No amount of projects and programmes and buildings and strategies will deliver the one thing that really matters.

I had given a Go and Grow presentation every week for the previous eight weeks. And I had now just announced the Go and Grow fund total of £1.4million. Understandably the reaction was one of excited encouragement - after all it is an amazing amount of money. The thing I was most encouraged by was not so much the total figure itself, but what the figure represented: the commitment of hundreds of people at St Bs who were prepared to give sacrificially to the incredible vision God had given us. I had encouraged people to give one-off gifts, or to commit to giving regularly over the next three years. It was essential that our people did not divert their existing giving to St Bs to the Go and Grow project. It would be a disaster if we funded a building project, but not the ongoing ministry of the church for which the building project was there to facilitate. Some people responded to this challenge by double tithing,

---

[53] 1 Corinthians 14:25b.

maintaining their existing tithe[54] to the ministry of St Bs, but then giving an additional 10% to Go and Grow. This was exceptional sacrificial generosity. Gifts ranged from a few pounds per month, to an amazing one-off gift of a quarter of a million pounds. Each was heartfelt selfless largesse. We had of course only just begun, even a vast figure of £1.4m only represented 40% of our full target. There was a long road ahead of us, but this was a fantastic start.

Now the initial push for the project was finished, and we needed to get going on the nuts and bolts: the legal contracts, the sale of our Holden Road site, and the continuing working out of many details. So, while at one level the project would become much more public, at another level a lot of the crucial work would now be done behind the scenes. I sensed that the project was entering a critical phase. From being a dream, it was becoming real. And with that there was a lot of hard work to be done and some hard truths to be faced. In all this we needed to keep our eyes fixed on the Lord and not on the project or ourselves.

---

[54] A tithe is a gift of the first 10% of our income and was the specified way of giving in Old Testament times and as such, is the cultural context for New Testament teaching on generosity.

Chapter 10
Exchange of Contracts

It had been almost a year since the momentous string of events that led to Topland agreeing the sale of Solar House to us, and by the end of 2014 we still hadn't exchanged contracts. What was it that led a hard-nosed commercial property company to stick with us? They surely could have achieved a rapid sale at a similar price to any number of buyers waiting in the wings. Yet they persevered with us.

The days leading up to Christmas are, for many people, marked by increasingly fraught exertions. Last minute presents to be bought, a whole new level of food shopping, writing myriad Christmas cards to people we never see, clearing out the house ready for the onslaught of relatives, and so on. Strangely, Go and Grow seemed to have picked up this eleventh-hour mentality, as if it were somehow infectious. After what had felt like almost endless frantic activity on behalf of the project, we were told that the deal on Solar House had to happen the week before Christmas, or it was all off. In the midst of this, I was also trying to keep up with Christmas as the amazing evangelistic opportunity that it is for the church. I was asked to speak at a community carol service at Saracens rugby club, with a congregation of upwards of a thousand; it was a great honour, but also a chance to present the gospel in a quarter normally beyond our reach. My head was spinning with my multiple roles.

The delays to exchange of contracts had all been on our part, as we struggled to demonstrate that the scheme was viable. The vendor had understandably lost patience with us and gave us one final deadline. What we needed was a deal on our Holden Road church.

When we started off on the journey, everything had seemed simple. As we ventured further into the project, the obstacles grew in size and complexity, until, utterly overwhelmed, I concluded that we were in the realm of the impossible. Quite early on we had been forced to acknowledge that we could not retain the North Wing of Solar House. Andrew Garwood Watkins[55] had bluntly stated "You can't afford it." Then later came the realisation that we would have to deliver the project in two phases. We simply would not have enough money to build the new church sanctuary in phase one, and so that would have to wait for a later date. Then, in the latter half of 2014, we wondered if we could afford anything at all.

The finances of the project were predicated on a lucrative sale of our existing church building in Holden Road. Holden Road is a leafy residential suburban backwater yet boasting its own tube station, Woodside Park on the Northern Line. There is a local park with the trickling Dollis brook, excellent schools and virtually every conceivable convenience nearby. As such, it is an extremely desirable place to live. Over the years the massive Edwardian villas have given way to blocks of luxury apartments. The old St Barnabas church stood in the middle of this attractive idle. The logic of the Go and Grow project was that the old church would sell for development for a hefty sum. However, this strategy proved more difficult to realise than I had assumed.

---

[55] Andrew, a surveyor (Associate of RICS), was a project board member representing the diocese.

The first prospective buyer that emerged unsolicited was a Jewish free school. Free schools were a concept dreamt up by the Blair government, to encourage the rapid establishment of new schools relatively free of the crippling constraints of education establishment bureaucracy. They were permitted to be sponsored by religious groups and were able to secure considerable levels of government funding. I had a first meeting with the school's promoters, to which Richard Greeves was unable to attend. I thought it went well and both parties were interested in a potential partnership. At the second meeting Richard was there, and he was not happy. "I should never have allowed you to meet these people on your own," he insisted. As it turned out there were a number of complications that made the deal unfeasible and Alma Primary School soon went off and acquired the old Whetstone Police station.

It was only after this abortive attempt to sell off-market, that the old church was put up for sale for redevelopment. In doing this we were venturing into a massive chicken and egg conundrum. We had not yet bought Solar House and so we had nowhere to move to. Church of England parish churches are not permitted to simply put themselves up for sale. In order to do so we had to have a viable plan to replace the church with a suitable alternative. And even then it was by no means a foregone conclusion that the Church Commissioners, who owned the church building, would allow the proceeds to be used to acquire a replacement. However, on the other hand, we could not make any progress in acquiring Solar House, our hoped-for replacement, without a watertight sale on the existing church in order to fund the project. Chicken and egg.

Initially, after conversations with people at the diocese we felt it would be preferable for the old church to be demolished. It was a fine building and held enormous sentimental value for us, but was not especially architecturally noteworthy. We were letting it go and at first it was felt that to see it converted to flats would be less preferable than having a cleared site. How often have you driven past a church converted into flats and thought of the decline of the church which is the invariable back-story of such developments? This was not our story; quite the opposite and we were keen not to have a false message proclaimed by obsolete architecture.

In November 2014 we started marketing the old church for redevelopment, asking for bids by 4th December. The moment the old church went on the market it became clear that there was no appetite for demolition amongst the developers lining up to look. It was regarded as too great a planning risk. The building was locally listed,[56] a non-legal designation that the Borough of Barnet had ascribed to it as a way of noting that this was a significant building. The planners would no doubt take the local listing into consideration and would probably not look kindly on a development scheme that involved the demolition of the building; at least that was what the prospective developers thought. So, the idea of demolition was dropped.

In our deliberations, we had been hoping for a sale price in excess of £5.5m. In conversations with developers a year previously, we had been given informal offers of between £4.5m and £5m, and that was without even

---

[56] This is different to a listed building which is designated by English Heritage at a national level (see chapter 3).

trying. A year had passed, and the market had risen, and we were now hoping for bids approaching £6m. At this level, the project could be shown to be viable. However, the old church was put up for sale without planning permission, so any prospective developer would be taking on a considerable planning risk. As a result, when the offers started coming in they were very disappointing, with bidding just short of £4m. At this level the project couldn't work, the figures simply didn't add up.

Would we have to go back to Topland, the vendors of Solar House, and tell them that we had a £2m funding gap? Perhaps we could plug that gap, given six or nine months, get planning and then get a better deal on the old church. But it seemed to me that Topland would as a result inevitably walk away from us and sell to another bidder. They had waited long enough, perhaps it was time to simply abandon the project.

After much deliberation and calculation at multiple meetings, it was decided that we would proceed with the purchase of Solar House anyway. We did this with the hope that we could achieve a higher sale price for Holden Road on the basis of a "subject to planning deal". This meant that the prospective buyer would offer a higher figure, but that the deal would only go ahead if an appropriate planning permission was achieved. Such deals are full of complexity and risk. We would have to proceed with a preferred purchaser without any guarantee of success. We would have to be involved in scrutinising the proposed conversion plans for the old church to make sure that the developer was being realistic. There was to be no clean break; we were unavoidably invested in the old church's redevelopment project.

At the very last minute, as if by a miracle, we received a couple of potentially credible offers on our Holden Road site and therefore got clearance that we were now ready. It would be some months before we eventually nailed down an agreed sale of the old church to a preferred bidder (see chapter 19). For now, we had at least an indication of a viable deal, and that was enough for us to take an enormous leap of faith and buy Solar House.

So, the exchange of contracts was set for Friday 19th December. Then, other factors contrived to stop the deal being done on the day, but thankfully the vendor confirmed the following Monday would be acceptable. It was now beyond the eleventh hour, with the clock inexorably ticking towards midnight. With nerves jangling, holding our breath, still the exchange of contracts lingered.

We urgently contacted the vendor's agent and said that we were now ready to exchange contracts. Now the pressure shifted onto them. It transpired that the property had been refinanced and approval to exchange had to be sought from an outside institution. With Christmas upon us it soon became clear that nothing was going to happen until after the New Year. However, the New Year came and went and still there was no news. The Champagne had been on ice for so long that I started to doubt that it would ever happen. What was happening? Had the vendors gone cold on the deal or, worse, been dealing with someone else? In the end the truth was far more pedestrian, a matter of mere administrative box-ticking that sometimes takes an infuriatingly long time.

The news that we were all waiting for finally arrived on Wednesday 14 January. We had at long last exchanged contracts on Solar House. When I heard the news, a wave of joy-filled relief flooded over me. A new horizon opened up, with something that for so long had felt like an incredible dream, taking one great step towards reality. A milestone had been passed and the scheme was alive and kicking. For a brief instance I allowed myself to just savour the moment.

Mere seconds after the elation of the exchange breakthrough, like the invisible aftershock from an explosion, I was hit by a second wave - this time of panic and terror. We were now committed and the enormity of the challenge ahead of us was no longer hypothetical. The trials of 2014 were to pale into a benign mist in comparison to the tumult that was to be 2015. The moment of faith had come.

Chapter 11
Problems in the family

It was ironic that very soon after the triumph of achieving the exchange of contracts we found ourselves looking down the barrel of a gun, perhaps even having to contemplate the demise of the project. The situation we found ourselves in was extremely alarming, and the worst of it was a sensation of being out of control, with the diocese calling all the shots. The project board meetings had become gradually more belligerent, as the colour-coded risk register turned increasingly red. I sat down and wrote a panicked email to our project board before heading off for a week's holiday. Others around me probably breathed a sigh of relief to have respite from their agitated protagonist. We needed to think seriously about how we would move things towards a more appropriate road ahead with the diocese.

Over the course of the Go and Grow project I have sat in endless hours of meetings. In order to achieve our objectives it was necessary to carry as many people with you as possible. In a church setting this involves huge numbers of stakeholders, as everyone feels the church belongs to them. All churches have to manage the careful balance between democratic accountability and forthright leadership, but in an episcopal church the breadth and scope of people involved is staggeringly wide.

Episcopal churches[57] are those who feel themselves to be all inextricably linked together, generally with their unity being expressed by the presence of a bishop. So, in the Church of England, for instance, clergy are not paid by the local church, but centrally, with funds paid in and out of a common purse. Each individual church has its own internal governance structure, in our case our PCC, but this is not separate from the wider church. No Church of England church exists on its own, it is always part of the greater whole. This is quite a difficult concept for those coming from non-conformist backgrounds, where each local church has considerable autonomy. At times it has also not been a particularly comfortable structure for many of us to live within. Sometimes we profoundly disagree with those to whom we are joined. But until a formal schism happens, this is the configuration of the Church of England.

Practically this meant that in order to proceed with this project we needed to get approval, not only from our local PCC, but also from the diocese and even from the Church Commissioners. We were never at liberty to go off and do our own thing. At St Barnabas we sit on the fringe of the Church of England; at one end of the churchmanship spectrum. In the past this has meant that we have often felt separate and different to our parent episcopal church around us. Over most matters of life and ministry, we have been left to our own devices, and have been happy to continue with very little reference to anyone outside our local setting. However, the sheer magnitude of the Go and Grow project made it impossible to continue to operate

---

[57] In the UK the main episcopal churches are: the Anglican church, the Roman Catholic church and the Orthodox church.

independently. So, I was plunged into a realm very foreign to me: Church of England governance.

Over the course of the project our PCC had many meetings, including several emergency meetings when we convened at short notice to deal with a crisis. I am very honoured to have served alongside an incredible group of people in the PCC, who tirelessly oversee everything we are doing with real scrutiny, whilst at the same time exuding faith. The Go and Grow project had been a long time coming and endless hours of work had gone into getting us to the point we had come to now.

The project board

The other main committee that had an even more hands on role in overseeing the entire venture, was the project board. This met literally dozens of times, sometimes in bizarre locations in order to make it possible for people to attend. An upstairs café in Paddington station, and a downstairs one in St Pancras station. But generally, we met at Diocesan House, the well-appointed main offices for the diocese based in Pimlico. The journey up the Northern line and across the Victoria line became very familiar to me.

Richard, Hannah and I would generally meet before going to the board meeting. Mike Vamvadelis, our church manager, would also come along to sit in on the meetings. Richard had been involved in the search for a new site from the early days and had been instrumental in pointing us towards Solar House. His involvement in the project had been pivotal to the point that without him one wonders where we would be. Hannah, an accountant who worked part time at a central London practice while juggling childcare for her two children, is another thoughtful person who was not satisfied to take things on face value. James, her husband, is also an accountant who was equally involved, but in another area of church life. Together they epitomise pillars of the church who were using their considerable talents to good effect. Mike Vamvadelis had been a South African Pentecostal pastor before coming to us in a management role. Back in South Africa he had led his church to build a new church centre just north of Cape Town and as such he was the only one of us who had ploughed this furrow before. However, the situation in the Pentecostal Church in South Africa is dramatically different to the Anglican Church in London, England. So, whilst his experience was relevant and useful, it was perhaps most valuable as a reassurance that these things are possible. Although Mike had been a successful church pastor, I always felt his talents were best suited to his role in operations. He relentlessly pressed into the details, asking questions that I would've skated over. Mike and Hannah acted as a brilliant foil to the gung-ho radical optimism of Richard and me, while expressing no less faith. Eventually, after years of stalwart service, professional commitments meant that Richard had to step back from being a project board member. He was replaced by Sam Markey, one of our churchwardens (standing far right in PCC picture 11.01) who often stepped in to chair PCC meetings. Sam was a brilliant thirty-something government executive. Having got a top degree, he had launched his career in local government, then moved on to central government and was working in the cabinet office at this time. He had a sharp, analytic intelligence that enabled him to grasp hugely complex issues and see shrewd strategies for ways ahead. He went on to work for a change management consultancy; I still have little idea what he actually did, but I was quite certain that the world is a better place for it. He brought a heavyweight brain, with the steady reasoned perspective of a Whitehall mandarin, to the project board at just the moment we needed it.

The other side of the project board was equally erudite. The project board's key professional was the surveyor Andrew Garwood Watkins, a middle-aged man with long grey hair which suggested a hippy past. Andrew was not an employee of the diocese but someone who volunteered his professional expertise. He was always something of an enigma to me; it took me a long while to work out whether he was for us or against us. In meetings he could be brutal in his assessments of our proposals. His knowledge of all property matters was incredible. I had never previously encountered this level of hardnosed professionalism in a church committee.

At the start, the project board chair was the then Archdeacon of Hampstead, the venerable Luke Miller. Luke, a graduate of both Cambridge and Oxford, had no background in property, but his searing intelligence meant that he grasped the subject so quickly as to often be ahead of the arrayed professionals.

The other project board member Andy Brookes, the entrepreneurial diocesan general secretary, under whose leadership the diocese had originally agreed to bankroll the project, moved on under something of a cloud. Another project that the diocese had heavily invested in had not been able to repay its debt, and the diocesan trustees were stung by the bill they ended up with. The project in question was a new centre in Tottenham Hale, which I had considered an inspiring innovation for the diocese to be involved with and just the sort of missional enterprise that we should be prepared to invest money in. Indeed, we at St Bs had put our money where our mouth is and given into the project ourselves. However, with their unrepaid loan, the diocese looked back and decided that the project had been oversold to them by an inspirational vicar, and inadequate checks made prior to the investment. Andy Brookes was the general secretary under whose watch this happened, and so he had to fall on his sword. And our Archdeacon and project board chair, Luke Miller, had been the inspirational Tottenham Hale vicar who had persuaded the diocese to part company with a significant amount of money. Luke had been tipped as a future bishop, but now made a sideways move to become Archdeacon of London.

Andy Brookes was replaced by Richard Gough, a charming and sharp-eyed accountant, with whom I had an improbable connection. Richard and his wife had some years previously done a season in the Alps, working for a Christian chalet holiday company. During that time one of their chalet cohabitees had been a young gap-year adventurer Grace McPhee. By the time Richard joined the project board, Grace was now our lodger at home in North Finchley and working as an intern at St Bs. Bizarrely, Richard and I were bound together by having had Grace as a lodger to both of us. Richard was also a regular New-Winer[58] and very much on the same theological page as us. He was, however, no pushover and in the project board we sat on opposite sides of the table, often through tense negotiations.

---

[58] Attended New Wine summer conferences and other New Wine events.

Andrew Garwood Watkins took over the chair from Luke and his place on the board was taken by the new Archdeacon of Hampstead, John Hawkins. John is a bright multi-gifted priest and he coped remarkably well with getting his head around the intricacies of a project that had been developing long before his involvement. But because he had not journeyed with us for the duration, I confess I was sorry to see the old guard go. Such was the longevity of the Go and Grow project board that a turnover of personnel was inevitable, but these particular changes also signalled a change in culture. Gone was the swashbuckling Andy Brookes; gone was the visionary Luke Miller and in came a new cohort of deeply cautious board members who were acutely aware of the diocesan trustees breathing down their necks in the wake of previously perceived impropriety.

Our new chair Andrew Garwood Watkins was also incredibly robust. When the Catholic Church proposes a saintly person for canonization, their life is investigated. During this process, one particular Vatican official is charged with trying to uncover any scandals or character flaws, lest an inappropriate person be inadvertently declared a saint. The inquisitor is called "the devil's advocate". Andrew Garwood Watkins consciously or unconsciously took on this role for us. Every aspect of the Go and Grow project was subject to his forensic scrutiny. He rejected anything that smacked of hubris or naivety, and when we advocated taking a leap of faith his verdict was contemptuous. Nothing got past him. So dismissive was he that it would be easy to assume that he was out to oppose the project. Yet it is important to remember that the so-called "devil's advocate" is actually a protagonist for the subject, but only after meticulous investigations.

Andrew Garwood Watkins was there to do the due diligence process for our project, and for that I am immensely grateful to him.

The project board was also attended by various other people and over its lifespan grew in number with those who, it was felt, needed to sit in on proceedings. Other people came and went; financial people, people from the property department, and our own church manager, all attending as observers, and contributing their own particular expertise. But one amongst these attendees, who was there from the beginning until the end, and was key to the entire project, was Michael Bye, the Diocesan Head of Property. Amazingly he lived in a village just outside Derby. His commute started with a drive from home to Derby station followed by a train ride into Kings Cross and then a cycle ride across central London to Diocesan House in Pimlico. Michael held a huge portfolio at the diocese and must've been one of the most overworked people I've met. He was remarkable at keeping up to date with his emails, done during his long daily train journeys, yet paradoxically at times could be nearly impossible to contact. This was his way of coping with the ridiculous workload placed on him.

As we entered 2015, having legally committed to the purchase of Solar House the stakes couldn't have been higher. It was at this moment that the changing of the guard took place and a new cautiousness overtook us.

Much of the work of the project board was to do with managing the risk. The Church of England is a naturally risk-averse organisation. The fact that the diocese had made an unprecedented, and seemingly reckless, decision to lend St Bs £9m, only intensified their desire to cover their backs. It felt like the moment they had resolved to

112

lend us such a huge sum, they were back-peddling, trying to find their way back onto the solid ground of prudence. And so endless hours were spent poring over risk registers and debating elaborate risk mitigations. There was detectable fear in the diocesan voices at the sheer enormity of the financial commitment. At the time the entire turnover of Diocese of London, by far the largest diocese in the Church of England, was only a little over double the size of our exposure in this one project. How had they ever agreed to this?

The PCC

We at St Bs were also coping with our own blend of faith and fear. We knew that this project could potentially shipwreck the church. The spectre of bankruptcy was a real threat if things didn't work out. Yet we also believed that we were following the leading of God and, as long as we kept our eyes on Him, we were able to continue walking on the water. At one late night PCC meeting we faced some bleak financial realities. With trembling hearts we voted on whether to continue the project or to pull the plug before it was too late. It would be hard to imagine a less daring-do group of people, huddled together in a back room in the old church, yet on that night this improbable assemblage showed unbowed courage worthy of a super-hero, pressing ahead in faith.

2015 was to be the most difficult year in the entire Go and Grow journey and I was ill-equipped to deal with it. The audacity of hope, the name of Barak Obama's second book, was originally coined, not by Obama, but by his

Pastor Rev Jeremiah A. Wright Jr[59] in a sermon, because for hope to be audacious there needs to be faith. At this point, I neither felt very hopeful, nor full of faith. Faith in

Pic 11.1 Our PCC in 2013.

myself had been pummelled out of me by the attrition of those meetings. Maybe that was a good thing, as the unseating of the 'God of self' is rarely done by a self-inflicted coup, but by external pressures. "How the haughty are laid low. How the mighty are fallen."[60]

---

[59] Audacity of Hope page 421.
[60] 2 Samuel 1:27.

Chapter 12
Planning: Early Steps

The acquiring of planning permission in a project like this is one of the key ingredients without which all other efforts would be meaningless. As soon as we had secured the purchase of Solar House and despite continuing huge attendant pressures on us, our focus needed to turn to realising our dream of a fantastic new church centre. One of the major hurdles still to be overcome was planning.

Planning pre-app

Even if we not been altering the outside of the property, it was a necessary pre-requisite of the project to get planning permission to convert the South Wing of Solar House from an office block to a church.[61] In addition, we also wanted to do substantial external alterations to the building: a new entrance, a small extension on the front, and a massive new church auditorium on the back. This process had started early in 2015. We had arranged to meet with the planning officer in a semi-formal meeting called a pre-app[62] on Thursday 5th March 2015. This was a chance to get an official reaction to our plans, with the opportunity to make amendments in order to give it a better chance of approval.

---

[61] Planning permissions are based on use classes, with offices as B1 class and churches as D class.

[62] Stands for "pre-application" and is a meeting prior to making a formal planning application.

A small group of us met up at the London Borough of Barnet's offices on the North London Business Park just off Oakleigh Road, not far from one of our church plants, Oakleigh Community Church. Slightly bizarrely we met around tables in the atrium café. I say bizarrely because this was a formal meeting, and I was a little surprised not to be ushered into a private conference room. Around the table was arrayed a formidable collection of battle-hardened property professionals: the Barnet principal planner who was to be handling our case, his assistant, our planning consultant Barry Murphy and his assistant Emma Penson, our traffic consultant Stephen Adams, our architect Jeremy Bell, and the Head of Property from the diocese Michael Bye. The planning officer took command.

He was tall and fair with a well-cropped beard, the epitome of a senior local government official. He had with him a slightly younger sidekick who was initially friendly and then, after all the introductions were over, said nothing for the next two hours of the meeting. The moment the planning officer arrived we all realised he intended to take control of the meeting. He was the power broker here and he knew it. He breezed in and announced that he'd brought his own agenda and promptly dispensed with the one that Barry Murphy, our planning consultant, had so carefully drawn up. Then, to further assert his authority on the meeting, he announced what he was and was not interested in and started to give the impression that he had already got the full extent of wisdom on our project that anyone could possibly want.

Having prepared something to say by way of introduction and make the case for the St Barnabas Solar House scheme, following Barry's agenda, I decided it would be wise to plough on regardless of what any newly introduced format to the meeting might dictate. Somewhat to my surprise, I was not only allowed to do this but was actively encouraged as the rest of the group visibly relaxed that someone was prepared to move things on.

Our plans were not without complications. Firstly, we had already made a PDR[63] application for the conversion of Solar House into residential flats. This was not a plan that we wanted to follow through on but it had been put in place as an exit strategy to ensure that the diocese could recover the money it had invested in the project quickly and easily should our plans collapse. This did not amuse the principal planner, who was not enamoured of hypothetical planning applications. At the time of the pre-app there were some in the diocese who were demanding that we make a full planning application for a residential development to shore up the diocese escape route. This would have been astronomically expensive in professional fees, for a project that no one wanted to see come to fruition. I considered it complete madness[64] and it was a relief to know that the principal planner was on my side on this point.

We intended to make one application to be delivered in two phases. By this point we had been forced to acknowledge that we would have insufficient funds to fulfil the entire project in one go. So, in phase-one we planned to convert the premises to a church, with all the accompanying works of: providing kitchens and toilets and new entrance and lift, etc. But not included in this initial phase would be the new-build works of

---

[63] Permitted development rights, see chapters 7 and 8.
[64] Thankfully this was not pursued.

constructing an entirely purpose-built 500-seat sanctuary church on the back of Solar House. That would have to wait until we had raised the additional finances needed for it. In order to plan for this second phase, we had also factored in what we euphemistically called "the camping phase". Construction of the new sanctuary would take around a year, so we pre-prepared elaborate plans to ensure the ministry of the church could be maintained during this period. The main Sunday congregation would move upstairs to a re-purposed first floor, the kids work would shift up to the second floor, and so on.

From a planning perspective all this would be spelt out in our application. Once approved we would immediately proceed to phase-one. Phase-two would follow at a yet to be determined time, but with all the permissions in place for us to be able to proceed at the opportune moment.

There were numerous factors that had to be taken into consideration. We were converting office space into a church. The principal planner pointed out that this involved the loss of employment potential. But the offices were empty, we countered, and in any case the church also employed people. He was unyielding.

Another major planning issue to consider was car parking. The fact that we were moving from a premises with just 6 parking spaces to one with 75 did not impress our phlegmatic planner. The moment we made our planning application, all mention of previous history would become irrelevant and we would have to prove our case from a blank sheet. But it was not only parking that was of concern but all aspects of transportation to and from the building. How were our church members going to get to the new premises, and what would be the environmental impact of all this travelling? The fact that they were all already travelling to and from our existing church was of no significance to this new planning scrutiny.

As the meeting continued, Barnet's principal planner gave helpful guidance and various of our professional team interjected their specialist contributions. There was no doubt that he was well prepared and knew his stuff and, despite his slightly frosty exterior, I began to think that this man could be an ally rather than a foe. Then right at the end of the meeting an amazing thing happened. I thought it would be good to end with a big picture statement of the overall vision from me. I launched into a pre-rehearsed speech about our vision for the regeneration of North Finchley, when the principal planner jumped in and finished my sentence, saying exactly what I had intended to say. It was very encouraging to find ourselves concluding the meeting with such a level of understanding and agreement.

Throughout the Bible we come across people who are not part of God's people and yet go out of their way to help the purposes of the Kingdom. Jethro the Midianite priest and Moses' father-in-law (Exodus 18), Rahab the prostitute from Jericho (Joshua 2), Ruth the Moabitess and daughter-in-law of Naomi (Ruth 1), Cyrus the king of Persia who authorised the rebuilding of the Temple (Ezra 1), the centurion who built the Capernaum synagogue (Luke 7), Publius the Maltese chief official (Acts 28) and many others. I believed that God's favour was on us and our project and that we were now experiencing similar such help.

Having navigated through the pre-app, we were furnished with all the details we needed to flesh out our full planning application. The principal planner, while not effusive (these people never are) seemed to be broadly supportive. The scheme looked possible. However, as time would tell, this generous first encounter was not to be repeated. Whilst I wouldn't describe this as a case of a wolf in sheep's clothing, we soon discovered that the Barnet planners were sticklers for inconvenient details, and we had many battles ahead.

At our pre-app meeting, the planners made quite a few suggestions as to what would be acceptable and what we would need to modify. We took these recommendations very seriously and modified our plans accordingly. Then we went back for a second meeting. At the actual meeting, with the new plans laid out, it appeared that the planners didn't have further objections. But the meeting was followed up with a formal report and that turned out to be quite another matter. It reminded me a bit of when Paul said, "For some say, 'His letters are weighty and forceful, but in person he is unimpressive and his speaking amounts to nothing.'[65]. The demanding written report usurped the previous more relaxed face to face meeting. So now, when we had thought we were almost there, a new critique of our plans added in all sorts of previously untackled details to be addressed.

The planning process rumbled on for nearly the two years. This stream of the Go and Grow story is picked up in chapter 21. In the meantime, the project faced other huge and potentially existential obstacles.

---

[65] 2 Corinthians 10:10

Chapter 13
Facing uncomfortable realities

I have often struggled with the many New Testament passages that talk of suffering. As I get up, in my comfortable leafy North London home, take a hot shower and munch my way through a breakfast of designer muesli, the niggling question is: do I suffer for my faith? Myriad Christians across the world will wake up to a very different world from mine, one where they are not allowed to worship openly, they are kept from decent gainful employment, left in wretched poverty, often ostracized from their families, and even in fear for their own physical wellbeing. Much of the New Testament speaks directly to these people. In comparison, my cappuccino being slightly tepid doesn't feel like real suffering.

However, when it comes to "testing", then I can fully identify with what the Bible has to say. In 1 Peter it talks about trials that are likened to our faith being refined like gold[66]. The Go and Grow project was such a trial.

When we finally exchanged contracts on the purchase of Solar House there was appropriate rejoicing that God had enabled us to get this far. However, once the dust settled, I quickly came to realise that the challenges ahead far outweighed the accomplishments so far. And now we were committed. The old adage that when it comes to a

---

[66] Peter 1:7.

cooked breakfast the hen is involved but the pig is committed, placed us firmly in the porcine territory. It felt like we had leapt out of the aeroplane and were hurtling towards the ground while hearing God calling after us: "I'll give you a parachute later".

At our project board meeting in February 2015, we once more looked deeply into the enormity of what God had asked us to do. The title of a famous best-selling self-help book comes to mind: "Feel the fear and do it anyway"[67].

1 Corinthians 10:13 says, "God will not allow you to be tested beyond your power to remain firm; at the time you are put to the test, he will give you the strength to endure it." (GNB). This passage is usually understood to be talking about temptations and is a warning to stay away from sin. But maybe it can also be applied to the faith struggles we all have. The repeated cry of my heart was "why does it have to be so hard?" Surely God would send us a multi-millionaire to give us barrow-loads of cash to take the pressure off our fundraising. Surely God would raise up a parade of cheerleaders on the Barnet planning committee to wave our scheme through without the murmur of dissent. Surely God would so affect the grandees at the diocese that they would suddenly be converted to the joy of a high-risk church project.

However, the reality of living by faith is a painful demanding experience. Gold is not refined by cosy warmth, and such was the temperature of the Go and Grow cauldron that I believe our loving Heavenly Father intended a precious purity to be a consequence. As our

---

[67] In the top thousand Amazon bestsellers, by Susan Jeffers, published by Vermilion.

testing endured, I took heart that God must have great plans for St Bs.

Now that we were committed to buying the property, we took the St Bs staff on a tour of Solar House. It was the first time that most of them had seen the interior of the building and the excitement was palpable. It was also the first time I had been there without a specific agenda, and it was great to spend an hour and a half wandering around imagining and praying. I found myself getting excited again and it made me realise afresh what a fantastic building it was. Everyone was impressed by the sheer extent of the space that it would provide. When we got to the top floor we were wowed by the incredible views across North London. As we scanned the horizon, we could clearly see Docklands, the City of London, the Shard, the BT Tower, Alexandra Palace, Wembley and Harrow on the Hill. The one thing that we could not see was St Barnabas. Even in the heart of winter, with no leaves on the trees, our current church evaded any sighting. I knew we were tucked away, but for such a large building to remain unseen was weird, like some elaborate magic trick.

A couple of things occurred to me from this experience. Firstly: January 2015 had been like no other I've experienced in my time at St Bs. For a number of years, we had started the year off with some kind of prayer focus, and whilst this had not been a fixture in the St Bs calendar, it had been an appropriate way to start each new year. But this year was different, as we found ourselves collectively holding our breath as we waited to see if we would exchange contracts on the purchase of Solar House. It felt impossible to see past this roadblock, and although many of us were engaged in fervent prayer for breakthrough, anything beyond this one affair was still over the horizon. However, the moment exchange of contracts happened, everything changed. We could now see far further than we had been able to just a couple of weeks previously, with a new vista emerging ahead of us. Like the spectacular views from the top of Solar House, a number of things, which were previously shrouded in the mists of uncertainty, had now become far clearer.

Secondly: Our move from Holden Road up onto the High Road and into Solar House would be a move from near-invisibility to remarkable prominence. Our current location was hidden and few outside the Christian community, even if they had heard of us, had any clue as to where we were. Solar House on the other hand was one of the most prominent buildings in North Finchley. Of course, hardly anybody paid it much attention, because offices are closed off private buildings that don't invite in the outsider. But, once a large new public entrance was created, framed by banners, it would be impossible to ignore, and it wouldn't be long before everyone knew where we were. How would that affect us and our ministries? We were surely set to change beyond what we could imagine.

The relentless tension of the project that seemed constantly to be in jeopardy was beginning to take its toll on me. I had an appointment to update our area dean. Paul was a longstanding friend, and I knew I would be received warmly. He had this uncanny knack of sitting quietly and eliciting a pouring out of my soul that I hadn't quite intended when I first walked through his door. Having fully apprised him of where we had got to, he said he felt that he wanted to bless me. I was moved and felt prompted to kneel on the floor. The moment I did so I

124

sensed a powerful touch of the Holy Spirit reverberating through my body the like of which I hadn't felt for years. Paul prayed and blessed and I knew that God was with us.

It was on a bright Saturday in early March 2015 that we had an amazing experience - we used Solar House for the first time. We held a day conference for leaders within St Bs. All sorts of people gathered: leaders of ministries, leaders of teams, leaders of missional communities. The day was packed with a full agenda of teaching and training. But what we hadn't anticipated was the remarkable effect that being in this building had on us. There we were gathering for the first time in what would ultimately become our new home and starting to imagine the future for St Barnabas.

Pic 13.1 The first time we used Solar House.

Most poignant of all was a time of worship. Someone commented to me afterwards that it felt completely different to worshipping at the old St Bs building. In one respect we had far more room. About 110 of us were gathered in a room that would've comfortably seated two or three times that number. Yet, counter-intuitively the worship felt more intimate, more connected both to God and to each other. The ceiling was much lower than at the old building, but because of the large windows on all sides, it didn't feel the least bit oppressive. Quite the contrary, we could all see each other, move around, participate, with no dark corners to lurk in.

Architecture has subtle effects on us. It communicates values, ethos and even beliefs to us. The old St Barnabas was a beautiful building especially on the inside. However, it communicated a theology that is contrary to the core beliefs and values of our church. Its neo-gothic architecture screamed at us that God is awesome but distant, that He reveals himself in mystery, and that faith is a private affair. To an extent all this is true. But at St Bs we have chosen to emphasise other aspects of our faith - that God is close and loving, that he can be known intimately, and that we undertake our journey of faith together in community. As such, ever since I had been at St Bs, I had found myself battling against the architecture, desperately wanting to tell a different story to the one echoing around those noble arches.

Whilst I loved our old building and would come to sorely miss her ethereal splendour, there is no doubt that this type of architecture is sharply at odds with evangelical charismatic spirituality. Worshipping for the first time within Solar House, even though it was still quite an unattractive and unmodified office block, felt like St Barnabas was finally coming home.

It was May 2015 and the Archdeacon and the general secretary of the diocese came to see me and Sam, our churchwarden. These were two of the most senior magnates at the diocese. The general secretary is effectively CEO of the multi-million-pound business that the diocese inevitably runs by virtue of its extensive ministries. The Archdeacon is the chief fixer for the Edmonton Area within the diocese, in whose patch we are located. You know you are in trouble when two such heavyweights ask to come and see you.

I, of course, knew why they were coming, or at least I thought I knew. The Go and Grow project was one of the largest church development schemes the diocese has ever undertaken, and in terms of diocesan financial investment, probably the biggest ever. John Paul Getty allegedly once said, "If you owe the bank $100 that's your problem. If you owe the bank $100 million, that's the bank's problem." And so it was with us and the diocese, and not surprisingly they had become very interested in us. But rather than become cynical and start pontificating about worldly motives, I welcomed the attention. Never before had I known such a level of shared ambition and partnership with our Church of England overseers or felt so supported both personally and as a church. One great benefit of working together with the diocese was that they inevitably came to the project from a very different perspective to us. This brought the wisdom of seeing things from a new angle and could be extremely creative. However, as is so often the case, the greatest advantage can at times also be the biggest frustration. We had a vision that we believed was from God and wanted to pursue it with faith, but the moneymen constantly argued about the numbers.

Jesus' most problematic parable is the parable of the unrighteous steward in Luke[68]. In the story, an unscrupulous manager defrauds his master when he

---

[68] Luke 16:1-13.

hears that he is about to be sacked, and shockingly the master in the parable commends him for his shrewdness. What is Jesus saying? We know from the rest of Jesus' teaching that he would never countenance either dishonesty or selfishness. Jesus concludes the parable by saying: "For the people of this world are more shrewd in dealing with their own kind than are the people of the light. I tell you, use worldly wealth to gain friends for yourselves, so that when it is gone, you will be welcomed into eternal dwellings."[69] If I had only read the second of these two sentences, I might have thought that Jesus was being sarcastic. I'm still not sure I fully understand what Jesus means. But perhaps he was using this story, of the most corrupt person imaginable, as a polemic to try and get us to be less naive when it comes to our worldly dealings. When it comes to massive projects and shed loads of money, we need all the worldly shrewdness we can muster.

The Archdeacon and the general secretary had indeed come to warn us that things were not looking good. Ever since we had exchanged contracts on Solar House just two months previously, the screws had tightened. Up until that point the risk had been largely hypothetical, but it had now become all too real. I knew we were on the ropes, with nowhere to go.

The enormity of the project finances were beginning to overwhelm us. Every way we looked at it, we couldn't afford it. The numbers didn't add up. The diocese had become increasingly twitchy, and whilst I didn't want to agree, deep down I had to acknowledge that they were probably right. We had a huge financial shortfall. The

---

[69] Luke 16:8-9.

dark clouds were gathering and try as we might to avoid the impending storm, there was no way around it. It felt like drowning in a sea, with no sight of land, exhausted and gasping for breath when we occasionally bobbed to the surface.

Chapter 14
Inspiring important people

So, how should we respond to the unfurling situation? We decided not to throw in the towel. All logic was pushing us to call it a day; to say that we had had a good go at making the project fly, but to no avail. As the saying goes: "better to have tried and failed than never to have tried".[70] In the end, I was gripped by an overwhelming determination not to give in.

Maybe in years to come we will look back on these days of heightened tension and trepidation over the summer of 2015 with a nostalgic gloss. In Hebrews 11 the heroes of the Old Testament are applauded for their faith, in language that suggests that they sailed through their challenges with graceful ease. However, if you look back at the Old Testament accounts of their exploits you get an entirely different picture of struggle, pain, setbacks and disillusionment, before ultimately coming through to victory.

The reality of our Go and Grow experience continued to be one of considerable difficulties. This was to be expected. No great vision was ever birthed in comfort. But take heart, God is on our side or, as the lyrics of the Chris Tomlin song we sang one Sunday morning that summer says: "If our God is for us, then who could ever stop us."[71] Despite my fears, now was not the time to lie back citing

---

[70] A misquote from Alfred Lord Tennyson's poem In Memoriam: "Tis better to have loved and lost than never to have loved at all."
[71] Based on Romans 8:31

"que sera sera." Quite the opposite, as with many occasions during this project's life, it felt like the final scene of Wallace and Gromit's "The Wrong Trousers," where Gromit, straddled on the first carriage, frantically lays the track in front of the careering toy train. For us at St Bs it would mean, not only a frenetic fundraising push, which would dominate our church life for the next couple of months, but also continuing along every other avenue of advancement available to us, without any certainty that the project could be redeemed. "Forgetting what is behind and straining towards what is ahead, we press on towards the goal to win the prize for which God has called us heavenwards in Christ Jesus."[72] In my best moments I knew that we didn't need to fret; we could relax, God was in control, and we utterly trusted him.

For many in the Church of England and in society at large, there has long been huge confusion over what "the church" is. A few years ago, I got given a book for Christmas entitled "England's Thousand Best Churches" by Simon Jenkins. I immediately rifled through its pages trying to find St Bs - surely we were in the top thousand! I was to be disappointed because the book was not about churches, but about church buildings. This is not just the perspective of the crusty establishment. Earlier in the summer, we hosted some Year 10 classes from a local school. We showed them some pictures of our plans for Solar House and asked them, "What do you think is the better building for a church - this one (our Holden Road site) or an office block?" Most of them responded by saying that the old building was better. When asked why, they all said something along the lines of "Well... because

---

[72] Philippians 3:13-14

it is a church". We in turn responded by talking about how church is a movement of people rather than a static building, using illustrations from the early church.

I saw our move to Solar House as part of a larger story that would activate the imaginations of people; would help them to grasp what church is and communicate to everyone in North Finchley and beyond that we are serious about reaching out to them and making them welcome. The very act of moving a church from a traditional brick and stone arched building to an office block was a polemic to the widely held notion that a church is a building. Some may struggle to understand this, yet for those who do, a new vista of what the church could look like will dramatically open up.

However, the misunderstanding around church buildings is rooted deep within our psyche; whether familiar or unfamiliar with Christianity, many people still struggled with the idea of what exactly church is. This is even true within the church hierarchy itself, with many of the internal structures of the Church of England predicated on an erroneous buildings-based understanding of church.

Being part of the Church of England, is to be part of something that is embedded in the nation. Often, the church has responsibility for buildings that are held in the public affection way beyond the immediate membership of a local church, and this has its stresses. An individual church cannot act purely on its own, as if no one else is interested in its internal workings, because this is rarely the case. Sometimes having to give credence to church organisational systems feels like an inconvenience, but it is there for a purpose. So, it was essential for the furtherance of the project that we were able to explain our buildings ecclesiology to those with influence.

The Diocesan Advisory Committee (DAC)

The Diocesan Advisory Committee exists to serve the local church in overseeing proposed alterations to the fabric of church buildings. It is filled with people who are passionate about church buildings, including architects and other property people. Inevitably some have felt that the DAC has conflicting objectives with churches; the one interested in buildings, the other in mission. But generally, my experience is that the vast majority of DAC members genuinely want to help facilitate mission rather than prop up mausoleums. The Go and Grow project, being aimed to provide an entirely new parish church, actually went beyond the normal jurisdiction of the DAC. Nevertheless, I was advised that to proceed without consulting the DAC would be impudent and it would not play out well should we fail to get their approval. The DAC was specifically interested in the auditorium, our main worship space, the area of the building that could be described as "the church". In particular, we needed them to consider our proposals for phasing the project, which was now an essential part of our project plan. The DAC had expressed concerns about the two phased approach that would not deliver an auditorium to act as the new "church" by a predetermined date and were reportedly going to raise this with the next committee up the food-chain, the SAC[73] and thereby with the Church

---

[73] Statutory Advisory Committee. This is a nationwide committee that reports to the Church Commissioners.

Commissioners. Potentially this could scupper the entire project.

So, we decided to invite the DAC to our proposed new building, so that we could explain our project to them. At the same time, some members of the Diocesan Finance Committee (DFC) had expressed a desire to see the building, so we planned to include them in the invitation. The DFC are in overall oversight of all the diocesan finances and in our case, without their ongoing support, we would not be able to continue with the project. They were in effect our bankers. To say that these two groups were important to us would be a massive understatement. So, the chance to show them around Solar House and share our Go and Grow vision with them was an exciting prospect for us.

Plans were drawn up for the visit. We wanted to treat them with the due respect they deserved, and I felt a bit of glad-handing wouldn't go amiss. We went to the considerable effort of transporting all the chairs up to Solar House and set them out in the exact layout we were anticipating for our future Sunday church meetings. Our guests arrived en masse, led by the Archdeacon and I felt a flutter of nerves as we ushered them into the ground floor. We had a promo video to play to the assembled DAC and the smattering of DFC members and then I addressed the gathering for a few minutes. This I did with gusto, sharing the vision we believed God had given us. I had clearly overrun my time slot as the Archdeacon jokingly referred to me as the "garrulous vicar". But the strategy worked. The DAC appreciated the trouble we had been to, and their response was overwhelmingly positive. Getting the DAC's support, whilst not theoretically a legal necessity, was a very important step in paving the way for the project.

Pic 14.1 Solar House ground floor laid out for the Diocesan Advisory Committee visit.

Bishop Richard

In early summer 2015, when the project was teetering on the brink, I was told that the Bishop of London had lost confidence in the project. What? How could this be? I had barely spoken more than a couple of sentences with Bishop Richard on the subject. The only way that he could possibly have lost confidence in the project would be because of what he was being fed by those around him.

Knowing that, in the event of a dispute with the diocese, final appeal would be to Bishop Richard, it was crucial that he heard our side of the story. I resolved to go and see him. Not wanting to do anything underhand, I decided to tell the project board of my intention to go and see the Bishop. This was met with a frosty silence, broken by the advice that this was an unwise course of action, and

I would be better to "keep my powder dry". I ignored them.

So it was that, at noon on Tuesday 28th July 2015, I walked up the grand staircase in the Old Deanery, Bishop Richard's London residence. Richard at this point had been Bishop of London for 20 years. It was widely rumoured that he could have had Canterbury but had turned it down. He was a personal friend of the royal family, famously preaching at the wedding of Prince William to Catherine Middleton in 2011, watched live by an estimated over 150 million people worldwide. He was a Knight (KCVO),[74] a member of the privy council and a member of the House of Lords. I had simply never in my life met anyone this grand. I stood as Richard entered the room and offered me his hand in welcome, with his characteristic booming voice. We spent the next hour, drinking tea out of fine bone china cups, with me explaining the vision for the project. At one point in the conversation, he said something that jolted my sensibilities and has remained with me ever since "One of the principal ways in which we sin is by being risk-averse". Far from "losing confidence", I left there assured that I had Richard's full support.

After my meeting with Bishop Richard, I reported back to the project board that the project had Bishop Richard's full support and was met with guffaws of protest "He would say that wouldn't he". But, for the briefest of moments, the naysayers were on the back foot.

---

[74] Knight Commander of the Royal Victorian Order; he has subsequently been elevated to Knight Grand Cross of the Royal Victorian Order (GCVO) in 2019.

Pic 14.2 Bishop Richard Chartres and me at St Barnabas in 2011.

Chapter 15
An engineering enigma

Our financial struggles and weakening confidence were by no means the only trials we were going through in early summer 2015. One of the most taxing and ultimately extraordinary episodes in the Go and Grow story was concerning the structure of Solar House. One of the early appointments to our professional team was a firm of structural engineers to advise on the building. They had undertaken a survey to look at the condition and it appeared that the property was robustly built. Confident that we knew enough about the property's condition, we had proceeded to exchange of contracts in January 2015.

It was only after we were legally contracted to buy the property that the firm of structural engineers made us aware that the structural loading requirements for a community building, which is the use-class D1 for churches, was very different to the requirements for an office block. Typically, offices are built to 2.5 kN/M² ,[75] rising to 3.5 kN/M², where subsequently fitted internal partitioning is allowed for. However, a community use building needs to be built to a loading tolerance of 5 kN/M². Community use buildings can sometimes be used for concerts and parties, and the floor slab needs to be strong enough to withstand the pounding of a packed room of partygoers all jumping up and down in unison. This isn't a minor variation, but a completely different

---

[75] Kilonewtons per square metre.

level of structural strength. The floor slabs would have had to be built thicker and with more reinforcement.

But now we had legally committed to buying the property. The people we had retained to advise us on such matters, the firm of structural engineers, had omitted to mention these loading requirements until after we had exchanged contracts. No doubt it was mentioned somewhere in the small print in their myriad-page survey. However, no one thought to remark directly on this engineering deficiency until it was too late. I was furious. Why were we paying astronomical fees to these supposed experts when they failed to advise us properly? Shockingly we had, it seemed, bought a multi-million-pound property that was entirely unsuitable for the use for which we intended it.

Unabashed the structural engineers now set about advising us what we could do about it. There was a way that the floor slabs could be reinforced using carbon-fibre sheet-layers applied to the underside of each slab. But it would be expensive, very expensive. Initial estimates put the price of reinforcing all the relevant slabs at £750,000. Discussing this at the project board meeting, a chilly gloom pervaded the room. I sank my head into my hands and quivered with despair. What were we to do? The finances were in a parlous position already, and this bombshell might be sufficient to wreck the project once and for all.

Something niggled in the back of my mind. Solar House had been built in the 1980s and was initially owned and occupied by NCR,[76] the office machinery company, as their UK headquarters. The building was so associated

---

[76] National Cash Register, a huge American corporation.

with its original occupants that it was known locally as "the NCR building" even decades after they had moved elsewhere. Was it possible, because the original owner-occupier would've had large amounts of heavy machinery, that the building might have been built to a higher loading capability than would be normal? Professional advice was "No", as heavy machinery is largely static, and standard office loadings are deemed sufficient. But chatting to Dave Harvey, our facilities coordinator, an experienced builder with a mechanical engineering background, we thought that the building looked more massive than would be standard for this type of building. It was improbable, but it was a glimmer of hope, and this flickering notion lingered in my mind and became the object of enduring prayer.

I raised the thought that the building might be over-engineered with the professional team, but the structural engineers were dismissive, insistent that it wasn't. I queried this "How do you know?" Their answer was, I felt, unsatisfactory. They basically reiterated that office blocks are built to a specific range of loading and that this was entirely inadequate for a community use building. So, they insisted, it would have to be reinforced. "But what if" I contested "this particular building was built differently?" "It wasn't" came the riposte. It was like speaking to a brick wall.

Despite my train of thought being regarded as spurious, I wouldn't let go of these notions, clasping at straws of hope. The structure needed to be further investigated, not least so that we knew more fully what reinforcements would be needed. We asked for test cores to be drilled. Weeks passed and I repeatedly asked "Have you got the test core results yet?" The answer was always the same; it won't make any difference. "Yes, but have you got the results?" Eventually, the core results came back, so I pestered the engineers to review them. They continued to stonewall, saying that it wouldn't change anything.

In June 2015, after what felt like an interminable delay, the engineers report from the test cores was sent through to us. I eagerly opened it, full of anticipation. Had God shown me that this floor slab, unlike any other of its

Pic 15.1 Test core.

kind, was strong enough for our purposes? But what was in front of me was entirely incomprehensible to anyone who wasn't an engineer. The detail was exhaustive and unfathomable, a cacophony of figures strewn across page after page of engineering gobbledygook.

Perplexed as to where to turn next, I got in touch with a civil engineer who was a member of St Bs, Michael Tan. My own father was a civil engineer, and so, despite my ignorance, I had always felt an affinity with the profession. My father had specialised in concrete, and how I longed now that he was still with us to help me at this moment. Michael, a quietly spoken Chinese-Malay man, married to former PCC member Jackie, stepped into the void and kindly agreed to look at the report. Michael's response to the report was not a complete vindication of my illogical stubbornness, but it did question the engineer's conclusion that reinforcement was inevitable. There followed a bizarre conversation between Michael and our consultant engineers, with me as the go-between. Discussion about sagging moments, midspans, concrete strengths, and geometrical dimensions, left me as a bemused onlooker in a foreign country. Occasionally I would interject with inane comments to the effect of: "Does that mean it's all OK?"

For some while the structural engineers stuck to their insistence that the floor slabs would all need to be reinforced. But with Michael's counter-wisdom, we continued to press. Eventually the case was passed to a more senior engineer and the tone markedly shifted, with comments like: "As you will be aware the design at this point is still in its early stages." The engineers had understandably worked to what were reasonable and long-held assumptions that this building would inevitably conform to normative standards. Any other conclusion was illogical and contrary to years of professional experience. But in the case of Solar House, it did not conform. Michael Tan had spotted that some of the figures used in the engineer's calculations were inaccurate and that those discrepancies made all the difference, to the point that most of the floor slabs would not need any reinforcement after all. The genius of Michael Tan had finally broken through this impenetrable barrier of flawed presumptions.

The conclusion was that the floor slab in the main building (not the rear extension bit) was strong enough for D1 use without reinforcement. The floor slab of the rear extension was of lesser strength, more in keeping with a normal office. However, this portion of the building was ultimately designated for demolition in our plans, and so not needed in the long-term. As we were looking at doing the project in two phases, this demolition was now likely to be deferred to phase two. So as a result, we assigned these areas to storage and office space during the phase one period. The only portion of floor needing reinforcement was the rear extension section on the ground floor, which represented just less than one fourteenth of the entire floor area of the building.

Bizarrely, this building had indeed been massively over-engineered when built 40 years ago. In a remarkable reversal of fortunes, the building that we had bought turned out to have been engineered nearly perfectly for our specific use. It was almost as if a prescient engineer back in the 1980s, ignoring all normal structural engineering conventions of the time, prophetically designed the structure with us in mind.

By July the projected cost of reinforcement had been adjusted downwards to £250,000, a third of its previous figure. By the time the works had to be carried out that cost had sunk still further to a mere 7% of the original estimate. It had become an affordable cost.

When I think back to possible scenarios, I wonder at God's amazing guiding hand through a series of the most improbable outcomes. Had we known that a D1 community building needed to be engineered to higher structural specification than an office block, we would never have bought the building. If Solar House had been structurally designed like any normal office block, the cost of reinforcement would have been prohibitive, and the project would have inevitably failed. The probability of this one building being strangely unusual and as a result appropriate for becoming a church, is so remote as to be discounted outside divine intervention. God was leading us, and through struggle and trepidation we were following.

But what happened next was to stop us in our tracks.

Chapter 16

The financial collapse of the project

By the middle of July 2015, the diocesan side of the project board, comprising Andrew Garwood Watkins, the Archdeacon of Hampstead John Hawkins and the diocesan General Secretary Richard Gough, decided to exercise their right and invoke the so-called parenting clause[77] in the relationship agreement. The business model for the project was collapsing, as the presuppositions it was based on failed to materialise. There was a £1.7m black hole in our finances and we had no conceivable means of bridging the gap. I vehemently disagreed with what I considered to be the draconian use of the parenting clause, but I was unable to marshal a cogent argument against the diocese's irresistible logic and so could do nothing in the face of this unstoppable conclusion. The figures were against me, and the money men would have their day.

The plan was to close down the project by selling Solar House. The only concession to this devastating news was that, for pragmatic reasons, they would not be putting Solar House up for sale until the beginning of September when the property market tended to restart after the summer recess. Tuesday 8th September was set as the deadline. This temporary postponement gave the

---

[77] See chapter 7.

narrowest possible window of opportunity to reprieve the project. If we were able to raise £1.7m from somewhere before 8th September, then the diocese would reverse the invocation of the parenting clause and the project could go ahead.

It looked hopeless. The sheer amount of money involved; the paucity of time for us to regroup, and all this happening over the summer when everyone would be away. Who had ever heard of launching a major fundraising initiative in the latter half of July and August? We had been set an impossible goal.

Facing what looked like the inevitable failure of the project, gave pause for thought about the entire efficacy of our vision. My mind trawled back over a journey that had thus far lasted a decade and a half. I looked back and wondered how did we get here from there? As soon as I arrived at St Barnabas I realised that there was a problem with the building and set about trying to find a solution. Initially we looked into extending and converting the existing building. We soon discovered that this was both expensive and unsatisfactory and so started to look for other alternatives. So, a strategy emerged to find a way of getting a new church building, hopefully at very little cost. The plan was to sell our very valuable Holden Road site, in its prime residential location, for a huge fortune and buy the much cheaper tertiary commercial site, building a new church with the profit that we carried over from the two transactions. I prayed constantly that we would only need to raise a small amount of money, if any at all, to fulfil the dream. Never in my worst imaginings did I think that such a scheme would end up costing anything close to the mind-boggling sums that our Go and Grow project was now projected to cost.

With the ridiculous target of raising £1.7m in less than two months, all was hopeless. I had pressed on regardless whilst, almost daily, I had faced with dread the nagging question: shouldn't we give up and pull the plug on the project ourselves? Doubts rose in my mind so strongly that I didn't feel I had the perseverance to resist them. Surely this was madness. I had never intended for the project to get to this financial position. Everything had run out of control and I was now presiding over the most extravagantly wasteful building project of all time, the very thing I wanted to avoid. How did we get here from where we started? This wasn't slippage, it was free fall.

Yet in parallel to these crippling doubts and fears, we had at every stage seen extraordinary things come together for which, outside of God's intervention, there is no credible explanation. How else could I make sense of the prophetic vision that led us to Solar House in the first place? There were the remarkable feasibility plans that our architects drew up, defying all expectations by meeting every single requirement we had thought up over the previous ten years. Or the unprecedented acceptance by the diocese of the plan for them to front-fund the project to the tune of £9 million. Or the fact that incredibly the parish boundary move went through without any major dispute. Or the fact that the property came onto the market just five days prior to us finally getting ourselves into a position where we could make an offer (and then asking for offers within two weeks). Or that we managed to beat off 17 other developers and buy the property.

Yet still I harboured nagging doubts that threatened to overwhelm me. What were we doing spending so much money on a building? It felt wrong. It felt contrary to all that we stand for; all that we hold dear. And yet I could see that it was also unavoidable. There is no other way of propelling the purposes of the kingdom in our area without decent buildings, not least this one that we were planning to act as a major hub for mission. So I was caught, not wanting to go down the route of profligacy, and yet necessarily being the chief advocate for this extraordinarily expensive project.

Several times through this project the word/picture had been given to me about Moses' arms being held up on either side by Aaron and Hur. Exodus 17 tells the account of Joshua fighting the Amalekites, while Moses was stationed on top of a hill, watching and praying. As long as Moses held up his hands (in prayer), the Israelites were winning, but whenever he lowered his hands, the Amalekites were winning. When Moses' hands grew tired, they took a stone and put it under him, and he sat on it. Aaron and Hur held his hands up – one on one side, one on the other – so that his hands remained steady till sunset. And so, Joshua overcame the Amalekite army.[78]

I had indeed felt like the tired Moses, barely able to keep going. I had known the reality of exhaustion in my walk over the last couple of years. Many had been the times when I had poured out my soul to my colleagues, confessing my doubts, acknowledging the paralysis of my heart in the face of such overwhelming odds. As I looked in exasperated fear at our puny attempts to achieve the impossible, I was given the response of life-giving affirmation of faith. There had been many more times when in my dejection I had remained silent and yet the Lord had visited me through words of encouragement and

---

[78] Exodus 17:10-13.

faith filled vision expressed by those around me, who had been like ministering angels pouring cooling oil on my afflicted soul.

I didn't know how much longer I could go on, with what was a manifestly impossible scheme. I didn't want to put my head in the sand and plough on blindly, because that is the stuff of folly. Yet the alternative was almost too disturbing to contemplate. Opening my eyes to reality was as excruciating as to gaze into the abyss; "We just can't do this. Lord help us! Please deliver us. Please deliver me."

I spent much of my time wishing the whole thing would go away. Or, if I was not allowed to merely wake up from an inconvenient dream, I occasionally even sank to hoping that it fully and finally would fall through. Maybe the guillotine of the September deadline would serve as a merciful release. We would have lost money, lost reputation, lost face and lost the trust of many. But at least I would be able to move on.

But the Lord was not allowing me to escape from the painful labour of faith.

The answer to the question: "Were we biting off more than we could chew?" must be an unqualified "yes!" The finances alone determined that. However, I had a deeper anxiety and that was: "Is the vision too big?" We've all heard of disastrous church building schemes that have resulted in half empty grandiose vanity projects. What was the guarantee that we wouldn't end up like one of those? Had we asked for too big a building? I questioned this because size is inextricably linked with cost. Why was the project so expensive? The answer inevitably being because it was so big.

The vision I had set before the church and believed that God gave us, was one of mission and growth. But my darker thoughts questioned this. Will the vast expanse of space be left largely unused; a hideous white elephant that had gobbled up huge resources and distracted us from the gospel?

Is the walk of faith meant to feel like this? One reads triumphalistic stories of valiant saints overcoming impossible odds for the sake of Christ, but rarely do these Christian bestsellers probe the dark night of the soul. It was spring and the birds were singing their loudest chorus. I was reminded of Jesus' words in Matthew: "Are not two sparrows sold for a penny? And not one of them will fall to the ground apart from your Father. But even the hairs of your head are all numbered. Fear not, therefore; you are of more value than many sparrows."[79]

---

[79] Matthew 10:29-31.

Chapter 17
I never wanted to be a fundraiser

This project had overcome a number of other impossibilities over the course of the previous couple of years. Faced with such a crazy objective of raising £1.7m in less than two months, I knew that this was one problem that I couldn't solve. Perhaps a little late in the day, I realised that I, as merely the vicar, was powerless to make this happen. I could not be the messiah of the Go and Grow project.

I presented the situation to the church. But instead of bemoaning our fate, as any sensible vicar would have done, in an act of reckless abandonment that I still don't know where I found the audacity to do, I stood up and challenged our membership to even greater commitment: "We all need to play our part, to examine our hearts and our wallets and to ask God how he is challenging us personally to respond to the predicament that we find ourselves in. And then we simply put one foot in front of the other and walk the walk of faith, totally trusting God for whatever comes." Inside I felt little of this faith inspired confidence, but I knew I had to keep going. God was sovereign and we are mere pawns in his plans, but whilst we had breath in our lungs, we were going to try everything we could to make the project happen.

The Go and Grow project was being tested and was now in, what can only be described as, its most critical phase thus far. Sometimes I looked at the challenges we faced and thought how impossible it was. Someone had recently reminded me of the story of Elijah on Mount Carmel when he challenged the prophets of Baal to call down fire on their sacrifices.[80] Having completely failed, it came to Elijah's turn to do likewise. But before he asked God to provide the fire, he poured vast quantities of water over the sacrifice until everything was utterly soaked, to make the fire falling challenge all the more impossible. Right now, I wanted to say to the Lord: "Please, no more water." Over the next few weeks, the project would be tested like never before. So, my second prayer was: "Please Lord, now send the fire."

Faced with such impossible odds, I had no idea what to do. As a step of blind faith, we decided not to give up, and so the only thing to do was to do something. Like the fabled Lemming, we resolved to put one foot in front of another, inexorably towards the precipice. We decided that we should approach a select number of members of the church to see if they would be prepared to effectively underwrite the project by pledging to provide interest free loans in the event that we had no other means of funding. I started fixing up appointments to go and visit members of the church who might have sufficient funds to be in a position to make a significant underwriting-loan. Of course, we have little idea of the true financial circumstances of our members. Some who have the appearance of affluence; a homeowner, a large car etc, are in fact living very hand to mouth with their outgoings often exceeding their income. Others, for all outwards appearances, may seem to have only modest means, and

---

[80] 1 Kings 18.

yet harbour vast investments. So, my approaches were largely speculative. A person who looked as if they had means got a call from me.

Much of the summer was spent going from appointment to appointment. Drinking copious amounts of tea, and occasionally something stronger. Talking vision and money to some people who hadn't previously fully bought into the project. It was hard graft and I hated it.

I never wanted to be a major fundraiser. In fact, quite the contrary, over the years I have always wanted to spend what money we do have as directly on mission as possible. I have consciously promoted the idea that we should spend as little as possible on buildings and by that I meant preferably nothing at all. The unspoken message was that buildings were usually a wasteful use of precious resources. In this I recognise that I was reacting to being part of the Church of England, which is the most buildings-preoccupied church on the planet. Everything in me wants to rail against such an attitude. Furthermore, I have watched many churches engage in massively expensive building projects that have taken up virtually the entire combined energies of the church, distracting it from its core calling: the mission of God. And yet, here I was fundraising for a building project so massive that all the other projects I had ever come across paled in comparison.

I've never shied away from making the big ask. But up until this point, the main challenges I had laid before people were about them sacrificing everything in order to step into their God-given destiny. This felt different. This was me pleading for money for a cause that most people considered to be my baby. A baby that had grown ever more hungry for resources and was beginning to look extremely corpulent, while in practice remaining on the brink of dying from starvation. My hosts were polite and gracious, and the underwriting loan pledges started to trickle in, but not at a rate that was capable of turning the project around. We were making progress, but it was looking like it was much too little and much too late.

Most of the time I hated fundraising. I longed to be released into being a fully-fledged minister of the gospel. But I had found myself embroiled in punting a cause for money. Was I prostituting myself and my calling for the sake of pursuing a project that, on a good day, I believed God had led us to?

Early on in the project we had had to reluctantly agree for the North Wing of Solar House to be sold on. We had hoped to retain the North Wing as an investment and as a means of being in sole charge of the building. However, I had become reconciled to the fact that the Lord didn't want us to keep nest-eggs for a rainy day but was calling us to follow in a walk of faith.

Potential proceeds from the North Wing were quickly added as a credit into the business plan for the project. A firm of commercial Chartered Surveyors were commissioned to provide a valuation, so that we could put a realistic sum in the business plan for what we could reasonably expect to receive from this sale. When the valuation came back, both Richard Greeves and I were speechless. It was over a million pounds lower than we had anticipated. We contested the valuation with the diocese but, with nothing else to go on, the diocese was insistent that this valuation be the figure put into the business plan.

Richard felt so strongly that the valuation was low that he managed to get the North Wing advertised in the Estates Gazette[81] at very short notice to test out the real market, rather than rely on a questionable valuation. This was the summer season when property professionals go off to Barbados.[82] It was for this reason that the diocese had decided to delay the marketing of the whole of Solar House, giving us the narrowest possible window of opportunity to reprieve the project. But now the same phenomenon was hampering this crucial testing of the market with regard to the sale of the North Wing. Despite this, it wasn't long before Richard secured an offer in excess of the valuation. It was still lower than we had hoped, but it was progress. Richard doggedly continued to press for a better price, and eventually was rewarded by achieving a price very close to his original estimate and massively higher than the professional valuation. The figures in the business plan could now be duly amended; a big piece of the jigsaw fell into place.

Whilst we were making progress, we had not yet bridged the yawning hole in our project finances. The 8th September deadline was just a few days away. I had received an incredibly generous response to my appeals for underwriting loans. But there was still a gap. As I prayed before leading our Sunday service on that early September morning, I decided to share our predicament with the church. I scribbled a rough calculation on the back of an envelope. To a silent congregation I delivered the disheartening news. We had faced a £1.7m deficit and

---

[81] The UK's main commercial property magazine

[82] I may be being tongue in cheek, but in my experience, a lot of property professionals vanish over the summer to exotic locations. It reminds me of the season when kings go off to war (2 Samuel 11:1).

now just six weeks later the shortfall was down to about £150,000. It was a miracle, but it was not enough. Slightly jokingly I said: "If you have £150,000 to spare, please let me know, because otherwise I'm not sure we can do this." As I stood at the back of church that morning a long-standing member walked up to me. His words are indelibly etched into my memory; he simply said: "You have your £150,000." This extraordinarily generous saint had in a single gesture closed the gap. Surely now the project could go ahead.

When I came to check the details, I realised that I had got the figures slightly wrong. We were still £20,000 short. The morning of 8th September, the deadline set for the final closure of the project and the selling of Solar House had arrived. We had done so much over the previous month and a half. We had come so close, and a mere £20,000 stood between us and our goal. First thing Tuesday morning is staff prayers, and I shared our plight. As we prayed together, I felt my faith levels rising once more and my heart warmed, buoyed up by the devotion of my colleagues. And then in what felt like a near repeat of what had happened on Sunday, one of our members of staff approached me and said that he would underwrite the final £20,000. I was dumbfounded. Astonishingly by 10.05am on 8th September we had made up the £1.7m shortfall. Solar House was now not going on the market, and we were going to be moving there. The impossible target had been reached. God had done it.

This represented a financial watershed moment for the project. Up until that September Tuesday every presentation I had made was prefaced by a statement to the effect that the project was so challenging that there was a strong possibility that it would fail. I was now joyfully forced to amend that preface, because now the assumption had shifted to be in favour of the project proceeding. The wave of relief was so strong that I almost felt faint with the intoxication of freedom to breathe again. But whilst it was appropriate to allow ourselves a moment to celebrate this milestone, we could not pause for long. The challenges ahead were to prove to be incredibly arduous.

After Montgomery's allied army defeated Rommel at El Alamein, there was great rejoicing. It was a significant turning point in the Second World War on which Churchill later reflected: "It may almost be said, 'Before Alamein[83] we never had a victory. After Alamein we never had a defeat.'"[84] However, at the time, in a speech at the Mansion House on 10th November 1942, a much more circumspect Churchill uttered the now famous line: "This is not the end. It is not even the beginning of the end. But it is, perhaps, the end of the beginning."

For us at St Barnabas, whilst we were still very much in the thick of the battle, the future had a more positive outlook. Richard Greeves, who had been an integral part of the project from its inception, now largely bowed out of the day to day business of Go and Grow. Richard, who had some while previously stepped aside in favour of Sam Markey on the project board, had continued to work tirelessly for the project behind the scenes. It would've been impossible to get to where we had without his incredible effort. His relentless faith-inspired

---

[83] At El Alamein, in north Africa in 1942, the Allied 8th Army led by Lieutenant-General Montgomery won a decisive victory over the German Axis Panzer army led by Field-Marshal General Rommel.
[84] Winston Churchill; Second World War vol. 4 (1951).

cheerfulness, even in the face of the most intractable problems, was a key ingredient in the project's success.

The Go and Grow project was a campaign to establish something incredibly constructive and life-giving in the heart of North Finchley. So, whilst the second week of September has left an indelible mark on our Go and Grow faith-journey, it was only one small step within the whole project. The overarching vision of the mission to reach North London with the gospel is of an entirely different substance; a horizonless venture that permeated both our present and future.

A momentous battle had been won, but there were more to fight just around the corner.

Chapter 18
The next hurdle

The diocese had agreed that the project was back on track. The parenting clause was rescinded, and we were full steam ahead. However, the ongoing urgent need for persistent effort didn't stop after the triumph of the extraordinary summer escape caper. The project plan required us to move forwards into the next stage of fundraising.

Through the autumn of 2015 we planned another fundraising campaign. A staggering nearly £1½m had already been raised from our membership. Now, just one year on, we had to do it all over again. I was having to go back and ask for more. This second campaign was to run over seven weeks, again spearheaded by me, with me giving a presentation almost every Sunday, although I was only preaching twice in the series. We needed to raise an additional £1m.

A million-pound target for a fundraising campaign is a colossal ask at any point. But St Bs church had already given vast sums in the recent past, and murmurings of *giving fatigue* were reaching my ears. This was going to require serious prayer.

One of the prayer events we planned was an hour of prayer in Solar House. When I arrived, I found Ryan Venn-Dunn[85] there with hiccups. He was scheduled to

---

[85] Ryan was on staff as our young adult pastor. He went on to train for ordination as a pioneer church planter and we joyfully sent him

lead the meeting and was looking a bit anxious as he grappled with his indigestion. So, I went in search of a glass of water for him. I went straight to the kitchenette on the first floor, but as I entered it, I realised that it didn't yet exist. I had been so immersed in the plans for Solar House that I had inadvertently, in my mind, projected the completed scheme onto the currently unconverted building. At first, I was disorientated, mentally insisting to myself that the kitchenette should be there. Then realising what I had done, I was struck with wonderment as if I had momentarily travelled forwards in time into our new environment where Go and Grow was no longer a future dream, but a current reality. What would it be like? In what new ways would we see the Spirit of God move? What would the place feel like? It is strange that an episode of hiccups should be the catalyst for a moment of revelation into the future.

We had a fundraising group charged with making grant applications, and this group included a chirpy, professional fundraiser called Matthew. Matthew was unremittingly positive, repeatedly coming up with ideas to break the funding impasse. And yet for all the shared optimism, the elemental figures kept crying out against us. Grant applications were slow in being made and then met with a depressing silence. Eventually, these applications did achieve some successes, with a couple of very significant grants. However, this was to take many months to achieve, and the work of the group was to go on for more than another year to come.

---

out in 2020 to be curate at St Pauls Mill Hill with the intention of continuing planting activities locally.

One of the grant applications was made to a charitable fund known to give to church projects that was chaired by a rural neighbour of my family, where my aunt used to farm. I chatted to our neighbour about our application and he promised to look out for it. The initial response from the charity was not encouraging; our project was apparently not what they were keen to fund. But then we received an email from the charity's executive saying that despite our project not meeting their usual funding criteria, their chairman was a friend of our vicar and so they were going to make the grant. I was thrilled. Sometimes who you know is important.

We were, and remain, hugely grateful for the very generous gifts we have received. But wild dreams of fabulously generous grants funding all our needs were just that: wild dreams. There is no fundraising silver bullet.

The fundraising campaign pledge Sunday

The fundraising campaign at St Bs seemed to go well. As we approached the final pledge Sunday, which had been set for 18th October, and in consultation with the project accountants, we knew that we needed to raise £250,000 in a single weekend. The diocese, whilst sharing our joy at getting the project back on track, was relentless in demanding that we keep going with the fundraising. The quarter of a million-pound target was not an optional extra, and we were warned that the project would once more be aborted if this objective wasn't achieved.

My previous hopefulness dribbled away and I was incredibly nervous. This was yet another make-or-break moment. Would we achieve it, or be cruelly cut off just as our confidence was growing? I announced this one-week £¼m target to everyone.

Pledge Sunday arrived and there was a great atmosphere in church. My faith began to rise that perhaps this was possible. The count was extensive and complex and took our office staff much of the week to conclude. The result of all the pledges from Sunday were emailed through to me on Thursday afternoon and the total came to just over £205k. I looked bleakly at the screen. I knew that this was an amazing amount of money born out of incredible generosity and sacrifice. And yet we had not made our target and this presented huge problems for the project. I was very grateful for all those who had given so much and yet I couldn't help feeling downcast. I sat there in silence wondering what would happen next.

Ten minutes later another email pinged into my inbox. This time it was from a philanthropic lady completely outside St Barnabas who had heard of our project and watched our video. She had been so impressed that she was emailing me to tell me that she was personally pledging to give £50k to the project. I sat there flabbergasted at this extraordinary largesse and at the amazing provision of God; perhaps we had made our target after all, and in the most unexpected way!

However, the £250k target set by the diocese was specifically for direct giving from our St Bs' members. We had other set goals for fundraising through outside grants. So whilst the incredibly generous gift from the philanthropist was hugely encouraging reminder that God was providing for this project, it could not be counted towards the £250k new St Bs' giving target. The finances were just about on track, but we still hadn't achieved our fundraising objective for that pledge Sunday and I was not confident that the diocese would allow us to continue if we missed this target. We had prayed for this; we had had faith that God would provide and that this would be a sign to us that he was with us, leading us forwards; yet it seemed we had just fallen short. I sat there momentarily conflicted, heartened by the amazing £50k gift, but disheartened by the shortfall and wondering what all this meant.

Then about half an hour later, I was still at my desk pondering these things and the phone rang again. This time it was a member of St Bs. "Henry, Henry, I'm so sorry I didn't get around to pledging on Sunday; is it too late to be counted in the total?" "No, no of course it's not too late." I responded "we'd love to include your pledge. How much were you wanting to give?" His response was one of those heart-stopping moments; he was pledging £45k! I sat, reeling from this, trying to do the mental arithmetic. We had very specifically asked St Bs to give £250k that week, and now the total of St Bs giving for the week stood at £250,084.50[86]. The wonderful gift from the generous lady from outside St Bs was on top of that.

The total for the September-October fundraising push was £1.16m, meeting our £1m target. We were rightly rejoicing at this amazing provision. However, only about £500k of this had been in gifts - the remaining amount being in loans which would need to be repaid in the future. We had manna for today, but not for tomorrow. We were still on that most uncomfortable of journeys, the walk of faith.

---

[86] It is possible that, at the time of calculating, not all the gift aid had been factored in, so the final figure may have been slightly greater.

Putting the fun back into fundraising

Over the following two years fundraising would continue, and whilst it never had quite the same make-or-break intensity of the autumn of 2015, it did become more personal to me.

For those of us called to lead churches, it is virtually impossible for us to differentiate between our profession and the rest of our life. I am not just the vicar of St Bs, my day job, I am also a member of St Bs, committed, passionate and involved. My entanglement in the church doesn't stop at a mere job. The church is full of my friends, and it has become my family. As St Bs church leader, I have felt like a parent to the church. Many vicars from a high-church tradition are known as 'father' by their congregants. However, as an evangelical, I'm not comfortable with the title 'father' because Jesus explicitly said: "Do not call anyone on earth father."[87] Yet, in contrast, Paul four times referred to Timothy as his 'son',[88] so Jesus' embargo is not as simple as it initially appears. So, whilst I don't go along with the "father" label, I do understand it. And parenting St Bs is not a job, it is a life vocation. My responsibilities at St Bs have never stopped at the office door, rather I have lived, breathed, dreamt and slept this calling.

When it came to fundraising, Jane and I felt we had to lead by example. We did so in publicly sharing how much we were planning to give.[89] But when we wanted to encourage our church members to go out and do fundraising sponsored challenges, we knew we should

---

[87] Matthew 23:9.
[88] 1 Timothy 1:2, 1:18 & 2 Timothy 1:2, 2:1.
[89] See chapter 9.

lead by example here as well. In the summer of 2017, we undertook two major fundraising exploits, one initiated by me and the other by Jane.

The Quad Bike Challenge

I had for some years used a quad bike as a means of local transport around Finchley. I fell in love with quad biking on holiday, much preferring them to their two-wheeled cousins, motorcycles. So, I had bought myself a second-hand road-legal quad bike and used it for local trips. Ironically a vehicle designed for rural off-road transport, I applied to urban roads, but it worked very well for me. I decided to use my quad bike for a fundraising initiative and planned a London to Lands End Quad Bike Challenge. The bike has a top speed of about 45mph and so we had to plan a route avoiding motorways and going on as few dual carriageways as possible. Jane agreed to be my road crew and was to follow in the car. We borrowed a trailer so we could bring the quad back easily. We timed the trip to coincide with New Wine and made New Wine at the Royal Bath and West Showground near Shepton Mallet our halfway stopping off point on a two-day trip.

I started the trip from the front of the Sunday morning service at St Bs, driving out down the central aisle inside the church. With Jane following, we spent the rest of the day driving along local roads through unnumbered counties. The throttle on a quad bike is operated by the right thumb. These vehicles are not designed for long journeys, and it wasn't long before my thumb was aching with the effort. I strapped it up with gaffer tape and wooden coffee stirrers and kept going. As we crossed into

Somerset it started to rain. Cold and wet I laboured on the last few miles and eventually rode triumphantly into the New Wine encampment, greeted by Paul Harcourt[90] at the gate and welcomed like an adventuring hero by the group of St Bs campers on our New Wine village.

Pic 18.1 Arriving at New Wine halfway through the Quad Bike Challenge

Exhausted by the first day I was slightly apprehensive about the second. I knew that I would struggle if the weather proved inclement. However, the weather was fair in the morning and as I rode off towards the Southwest, the sun came out. It was a glorious day with the highlight being riding over Dartmoor. Tired, aching, but satisfied, I made it to Lands End, followed by my faithful road crew: Jane. We had raised over five thousand pounds for Go and Grow.

---

[90] National Leader of New Wine.

The Barn Dance

Jane's fundraising idea was to throw a party. In March 2017 we had our 33rd wedding anniversary. March is not the best time to hold a party, especially if you want it to be outside. We calculated that the summer of 2017 would mark exactly a third of a century married for us, a perfect reason for a celebration. So, we started to make plans for a tricentennial wedding anniversary party. Not surprisingly most people didn't properly understand the concept, but that didn't matter. We had the use of an historic, although rather decrepit, barn at a farm in Buckinghamshire belonging to our family. So, we decided to have a barn dance in the old barn and in the surrounding farmyard. On Saturday 23rd June it was a balmy summer's evening with over a hundred guests gathered at the farm in high spirits. Part way through the

Pic 18.2 Barn Dance in full swing.

evening, our associate Vicar Colin Brookes conducted an auction of just five lots, some of which attained suitably crazy prices. One of the lots Jane and I had donated was a bottle of vintage claret. It was a good wine, but hardly justified the hammer price of £330. The high bidders that evening tended to be our non-St Bs friends and family who relished their first chance to support the project. By the end of the day, we had had enormous fun and astonishingly raised over ten thousand pounds.

Another benefit of the fundraising feats that Jane and I had engaged in was to reinforce the fundraising agenda in and around St Bs. We wanted to put the "fun" back into fundraising, and in this we felt we had succeeded. That said, our efforts, combined with all the other exploits of St Bs members, raised only a small proportion of the total. The vast majority of money raised for the project came from direct giving. The incredible generosity of St Bs members remains one of the most remarkable aspects of this project.

Chapter 19
Selling a church

Proverbs 4:18-19 - "The path of the righteous is a blazing light which increases in intensity until the day is full, but the way of the wicked is black pitch and littered with obstacles which foul the feet."

Much history had passed in the last few months. Our initial optimism had been tested in the cauldron of the brutal commercial realities. Many times we had wondered if the entire project would collapse, as time and again it proved to be more challenging than we could possibly have imagined. Gigantic obstacles appeared to litter our path. The proverb has two paths; were we on the right path? In my prayers I was transported back three and a half years to the January 2013 prayer meeting that initiated the whole Go and Grow adventure. However difficult the path was to be, the words given at that historic prayer meeting about being "a blazing light," were an affirmation that the answer was yes.

Whilst we had made huge strides, the obstacles in our path had not all gone away. Indeed, as soon as one hurdle was overcome another came in to replace it. The attrition was relentless. And now, in the immediate future ahead of us were a number of major property transactions. In all the dealings of the Go and Grow project, the one that I had had most experience of in my previous profession as a surveyor was sales, as for nearly ten years I had worked as an estate agent selling property. Yet surprisingly, it was in this area that I felt least equipped and most unsettled. For me, a former area of strength felt like it had become a weakness. Nevertheless, the project required us to sell four properties.

13 Courthouse Road was a house the church had owned for many years, and whilst it had been used for housing clergy at various points, it was now let out and was therefore, in effect, acting as an investment property. It would have been helpful to us to keep this property, but the financial realities of the project didn't allow for this. The business plan needed the proceeds of this property and so it had to be sold.

76 Old Farm Road was a three bedroomed duplex apartment on the Strawberry Vale Estate. It had been a gift by an extraordinarily generous couple who had been at the heart of St Bs for a number of years but had now retired and moved away to the shires. Strawberry Vale was where we had planted a church five years previously, and this had grown and was doing very effective ministry around the estate. The apartment had been used to house various volunteers, on the basis of a flat share. Like Courthouse Road, this was a useful property, which we would have loved to have retained, but at this point, it was surplus to our requirements, and we needed the money more than the property; so it had to go.

The two other properties to be sold were of an entirely different nature: our existing church in Holden Road and the North Wing of Solar House.

St Barnabas Church in Holden Road had been our parish church for 101 years. We had celebrated the centenary eighteen months before in March 2014 and had been delighted to welcome the now very elderly daughter of the first vicar the Reverend Henry Goulden Phillipson, to join us for those celebrations. But now this magnificent church building was to be sold. Many, myself included, approached this moment with an undeniably heavy heart.

Pic 19.1 St Barnabas' missioner and first vicar: Reverend Henry Goulden Phillipson (centre right) at the laying of the foundation stone in 1912. His daughter joined us for the centenary celebration in 2014.

Initially when we started marketing the church, we had received bids from developers without planning permission. This meant that a developer would buy the church on the basis that they took all the planning risk. If they went on to achieve a desirable planning approval, they would make a considerable return for the risk they had taken. On the other hand, if they failed in the planning bid, they would be landed with an undevelopable church that they had no use for. Not surprisingly, the offers tendered on this basis were low; far beneath what we needed to achieve our aims. Therefore, we resolved to sell subject to planning, where the developer buying the property proceeds to apply for planning, but need only complete the purchase and pay over the money should the planning application be successful. Early in 2015, we had finally managed to agree the sale of the old church to a preferred bidder, a developer called "Paradigm", subject to planning.

Selling a parish church is a highly complex process at the best of times. As incumbent vicar, I was said to "own the freehold". But for ecclesiastical property, the vicar "owning the freehold" doesn't mean the same thing as a normal private individual owning his or her own home. I couldn't just sell it; although it legally had my name against it, in practice it was really owned by the Church Commissioners. They in turn would only countenance the sale of a parish church in very rare and specific circumstances; if the church was being closed down, or if a suitable alternative parish church was being provided. We fell into the latter of those two categories, and it had now been agreed that the Solar House project would provide a suitable alternative parish church. Part of the process of demonstrating that our plans constituted a suitable replacement church had been the hosting of the

DAC (see chapter 16), who whilst not legally required to approve the project, had been hugely influential.

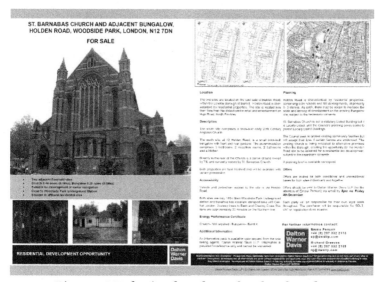

Pic 19.2 Marketing brochure for the church.

In practice we had to close the old St Barnabas through a process called "making the church redundant", only to then reopen an entirely new parish church at Solar House. Most churches that are made redundant are being closed because of decline and failure to grow the church for the new generation. Our story was very different, but this story of life and growth needed to be repeatedly explained to the various overseeing parties, whose assumption was commonly that the church was sadly being shut down. The entire legal procedure of the project was governed by a deed originating from the Bishop of London called a Pastoral Measure. There was nothing particularly pastoral about this document; it simply spelt out the basis of the project to relocate our parish church.

The timings of the transactions were complicated, with multifarious factors needing to be taken into account. We wanted to retain occupancy of our existing church building until the conversion works at Solar house had been completed, so that we could finish our worship services one week at the old church and commence them the next week at the new one. At the same time, several other factors needed to come into alignment: the developer's planning application on the existing church, our planning application on Solar House, the sales of all the other properties and the contract to do the conversion works to Solar House.

To achieve a perfectly synchronised smorgasbord of diverse factors, we needed to work closely with the developer Paradigm and their two senior executives. Rarely have I experienced such a clash of cultures than over this relationship. When we initially started to treat with Paradigm we had dealt with a charming Totteridge gentleman, who I was told was the money behind the project. I found him to be polite and gracious and gave a strong impression that he deeply appreciated the aesthetic of this beautiful building. I came away from a meeting with him reassured that our precious building would be treated sympathetically. He also had the reputation of having deep pockets. However, it was not long before this senior statesman faded from view, and we found ourselves dealing with two senior directors of the company.

The culture in the church has become far more professional than it was a generation ago. Dealing with the executives at the diocese had been extremely demanding and our negotiations with them had been quite exacting. But working with the diocese was a *walk in the park* compared with the ruthless world of property development. Dealing with our purchaser, some of the aggressive tones used towards our staff were certainly not what we were used to and I considered it to be an unacceptable way to conduct business with anyone, let alone a church. It sometimes felt like an onslaught.

The deal had eventually gone through and we had exchanged contracts, but the frictions continued. As dialogue became fraught, I came to wonder how we got here. Were these really the sort of people we wanted to sell to? But they now had a legal stake in the property, and we could no longer dismiss them as an inconvenience. Our church building was no longer wholly ours to do what we liked with, because we had contracted to sell it to them. So, an uncomfortable period ensued including the most fractious dealings I have ever experienced in all my years of observing property transactions[91].

With my confidence in the propriety of the purchaser shaken, I was left with nervousness about what these developers would end up doing to our wonderful building. Since then, I have watched the progress on the site with considerable interest. Were these developer-bruisers going to extend sufficient respect to the majestic old church? In the end I have to admit that I needn't have feared. The Barnabas development is a triumph. The building looks beautiful and the pictures I've seen of the interiors of the apartments look spectacular.

The North Wing of Solar House was to be another complex and convoluted sale. One of the initial bidders had been the developer of our Holden Road church. With

---

[91] The ongoing story of this sale is told in chapter 23

this approach, we were minded to seize the opportunity to simplify the entire project. With the same purchaser for both properties we would be potentially reducing the risk of the various sales not meeting the exacting timescales that we needed. However, negotiations hit the buffers when it came to stairs. We needed to be able to use the main stairs in the North Wing as our fire escape. This was not acceptable to the developer who intended to convert the property to residential flats.

Pic 19.3 Presentation slide explaining the North Wing.

At this point another purchaser emerged. The main tenant in the North Wing expressed a desire to buy the property that they were currently renting. This purchaser was not a developer but was in the business of providing high quality serviced offices. This deal needed no planning changes and the stair issues were easily resolved. Negotiations over parking spaces took a while but were eventually resolved as well. So, we ended up with a far more satisfactory neighbour, with whom we got on well. Having two side-by-side owners in the same building adds many complexities over shared access, common parts and shared HVAC.[92] These potentially thorny issues were to be the subject of a detailed service charge to be administered by an outside consultant. Despite these tricky arrangements, I'm pleased to say that this sale caused few of the headaches that the sale of the old church had done and went through satisfactorily and on schedule.

It had been a nail-biting year. The entire project was dependent on these four property sales all going through at the right time and at the right price. We were inevitably entirely reliant on our purchasers; people who we didn't know and at some points didn't really trust. I found it all quite frightening, as we were not in control of our own fate; but then the idea that we are ever in control is largely an illusion, born of over focus on self. Despite the asphyxiating jeopardy of the journey, we were and always had been, in the safe hands of God.

---

[92] Heating Ventilation and Air Conditioning. Strictly speaking the system at Solar House is not full air conditioning, but "air handling". However, this does include both heating and cooling of the air, so the difference is largely semantic.

Chapter 20
The Pastoral Committee

Right from the beginning of the project we had spent a lot of time and energy trying to keep our membership appraised of our plans as they unfurled. This was quite a difficult exercise, as the project had such a lot of uncertainties, it was often very problematic to know what to communicate. Nevertheless, we did our best trying to keep everyone informed, even though the project's ponderous speed meant that there were long periods when we had very little to say.

I was initially mainly concerned about the response of the local community, as we had done none of our planning in a corner, and the goals we were pursuing were widely known. So, I thought it possible that we might receive quite a backlash from local residents and heritage zealots. However, at least at this juncture of the project, I was wrong. The first opposition came from within.

In a church, the size of St Barnabas, with well over a thousand people on the database, there are inevitably a large range of views, so objections were unavoidable. Amazingly, in the event, we received just one objection. My immediate response was elation, it appeared that the vast majority of our membership had bought into the vision, and that there was no groundswell of opposition to the project. Just one solitary objection. But in the Church of England's ultra-cautious approach, every single view had to be fully taken into consideration. One objection was all that was needed to trigger the full appeals process.

The person who tabled the objection was a long standing and well-respected member of the church. He was retired and he and his wife took an active part in a small group and in other activities. He had shown great interest in the project and he and I corresponded regularly. I found his lengthy letters generally helpful and informative. But it was clear that, whilst he could see that we needed to do something with our buildings, he remained unconvinced that the scheme we were pursuing was the right approach. I'm not sure he fully anticipated what his objection initiated, because what followed was a formal legal process leading to a form of judicial hearing called a "pastoral committee"[93].

A maelstrom of activity was mounted to prepare for this challenge involving copious reports and papers being generated to explain the particulars of the project and processes that had been involved in getting this far. The project board met, and it was decided that Michael Bye (the Diocesan Head of Property), the Archdeacon and I would represent the project for St Barnabas and for our partners, the diocese. It was at this moment that I was most grateful for all the help we were receiving from the diocese. Despite the tensions of our stop-go progress throughout 2015, it was clear that they now were fully on board and had our back. There would also be one other person speaking on our behalf, Franklin Evans. Franklin, a barrister, had been the original chair of the building development group over a decade ago and was a current member of our Standing and Finance Committee. But on that day, he would be speaking as a private individual

---

[93] A bit like the pastoral measure (see chapter 19) there was nothing particularly pastoral about this committee. Another classic Church of England misnomer.

member of the church. It was poignant that he was also a close friend of the gentleman who had made the objection.

Knowing that this would be make-or-break, I had very little sleep the night before; my mind was racing about parking spaces and PCC deliberations. I got up, showered and put on a suit and dog-collar. I needed to look my best for my "day in court".

So it was that on Wednesday 9th December 2015, at 10.30 am, I, along with others, was summoned into a committee room in Church House[94] in Westminster to appear before the pastoral committee. The hearing was to last one hour, and the conclusion would be that the committee would rule whether or not the project would be allowed to go ahead.

The hearing followed a similar format to what I imagine government committees do, which one occasionally sees snippets of on the news. At the end of a corridor was a rather plain room furnished with a horseshoe table, behind which was arrayed a panel of experts. In front of the horseshoe was a rectangular table with three seats. This was where we were to make our presentation and be questioned. Behind was the public seating, where anyone who wanted, could come and observe the proceedings; this is where our little group initially came in and sat.

First the one complainant spoke briefly and was asked questions. He had two main arguments against the project.

---

[94] The headquarters of the Church Commissioners in central London, next to Westminster Abbey.

His first point was about parking. The old church was in a residential road with derestricted free parking on Sundays. We only had six off-road parking spaces on the front forecourt of the church, so practically everyone parked in the road. There is no doubt that this was quite convenient for us, but it also riled the local residents. Inconsiderate parking or too much traffic gridlocking the road, were regular features of Sundays. And I found myself constantly apologising to angry neighbours. The new building had 77 parking spaces, and despite this being a massive increase in our capacity, we knew that this would quickly fill up and we would have to manage the situation very carefully. The 230 space Lodge Lane Car Park was to be only four minutes walk down the High Road, and from experience was largely empty on Sundays. So, this had to be part of our solution. The gentleman complainant didn't see it this way. He thought that our current Holden Road parking situation was excellent and that we would be causing ourselves huge parking problems by the move.

His second point was that we shouldn't be spending our money this way. Instead, we should be investing our money in deploying interns. I had some sympathy for this view, because I had always balked at the sheer cost of the project. Conversely, I also wanted St Bs to be a major centre for training and raising up new talent. In the past we have had as many as a dozen interns working with us at a time, and I longed to see those days return. We had put our internship programme temporarily on hold largely because of the lack of capacity, which had been caused by the capacity-draining Go and Grow project. The project had become a ravenous monster, devouring everything we could throw at it. So, as I sat and listened to this gallant complainant, I couldn't help but agree with him. However, this was a quasi-legal hearing, and his points did not amount to a cogent legal reason why the project should be terminated. We had duly considered all aspects of the project, looked into issues of parking, and thought about alternatives. All this had been the subject of thorough consultations. So, in the end his arguments didn't stack up.

It became abundantly clear that all members of the committee had meticulously read all 174 pages of the supporting papers and were very well informed. Their questioning was sharp, and they were conversant with all the relevant facts. The complainant floundered, apologising for not being adequately eloquent. I would have felt sorry for him being subjected to such a gruelling interrogation, but I was aware that in a very few minutes it would be me in that hot seat. I doubted that the panel would show me more mercy than it had him.

The next person summoned to speak was our barrister friend Franklin Evans. Franklin spoke in support of the project, again followed by some questions. Honed by years of courtroom discourse, Franklins oratory was immaculate. But I knew that the wily members of the panel would not be swayed by fluent rhetoric, and at this point had no idea which way the case was going.

Finally, three of us: the Diocesan Head of Property, the Archdeacon and I, were summoned to take to the stand. I was grateful that Michael Bye, the Head of Property, took the lead, he having spoken at this type of hearing many times before. Occasionally, I was invited to comment on, or clarify certain issues. There was a lot I wanted to say, but I knew that I had to stick scrupulously to the specific subject being addressed. Almost as soon as it had begun, our bit was all over, and we were asked to go and wait in a separate room for the committee to deliberate.

All of us who had spoken now stood around in this small anteroom. The atmosphere was awkward, as the gentleman who had spoken against the project was clearly embarrassed to be there with the rest of us. What does one talk about, the weather?

After a short wait, pregnant with hope and anxiety, we were invited to return to the committee room for the committee's conclusion. In a couple of minutes, the chairman summed up their conclusion, which was to allow the scheme to proceed. A wave of relief washed over me. Breath returned to my being, as I whispered a heartfelt "Thank you" to the Lord. For a time, it had felt like the entire future of St Bs had hung in the balance, but now a major hurdle had been passed. The process had been incredibly thorough, gruelling and nerve-jangling. The resulting assent had left me exhausted but happy that we were still in the game.

Many more hurdles were still ahead of us, and the sheer scope of the project had become so complex that we felt that we were beginning to lose control. I couldn't help feeling that another crisis was just around the corner, and that we were ill-prepared to meet it.

Chapter 21
Professionals and project management

For a project of this size, we inevitably needed a large professional team. We had already got some of the key players in place: project managers, architects, planning consultants, QS[95], structural engineers and traffic consultants. But as the project advanced more specialist consultants also needed to be engaged and the pre-app had served to highlight some of the gaps we hadn't yet addressed. I have spent quite a bit of time in and around the property world, but even I was boggled by the enormity of this emerging team. We went on to appoint: acoustic consultants, M&E[96] consultants, BREEAM[97] and energy consultants, transport consultants, a sunlight-daylight consultant[98] and finally, a communication consultant. I had never previously heard of a number of these specialisms, and it made me wonder what other professional consultants we would need: a "depth of shag-pile carpet consultant," or a "how to clean the windows consultant?"

Things that we needed to take into consideration included: noise, environmental impact and the massing of

---

[95] Quantity Surveyor.
[96] Mechanical and Electrical.
[97] Building Research Establishment Environmental Assessment Method.
[98] More commonly called a "rights of light" consultant.

the new auditorium at the back. The rights of light consultant we had engaged was commissioned to do computer modelling for us. In the event, our rights of light consultant was able to demonstrate ample room and our architects were able to design a fantastic new sanctuary within the specified massing envelope.

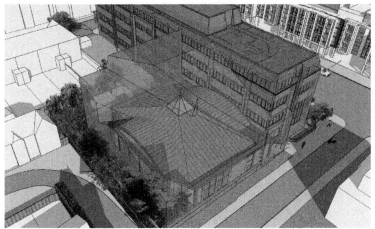

Pic 21.1 3D CGI drawing of rights of light massing envelope (see grey box over planned new church sanctuary).

Throughout the tumultuous year of 2015 we made small steps of progress in some directions, while other areas looked bleak. Cracks had begun to appear. Many of the people involved were under incredible strain. Professional fees were threatening to run out of control.

After 25 years in church leadership, I had found myself thrust back into the cut-throat world of commercial negotiation and professional advisors. This had been more of a shock than I anticipated. Having worked in a professional environment for many years I had expected to fit back in without too much difficulty. But I have found that many of the practices that the commercial world treat as entirely normal, are quite foreign to the church and charity sector and vice versa. There is a stark clash of cultures.

The most obvious manifestation of this clash was with regards to money. Within the church we are used to making our money stretch a very long way. For instance, given ten thousand pounds we might use it for employing someone for up to six months, who would gather around them a proficient team of volunteers and go on to make a lasting impact on the lives of numerous people. Yet in the professional world such a sum vanishes in little more than an instant with the writing of a few letters and attendance at a couple of meetings. I live daily with the knowledge that every penny received by St Bs might be at the cost of couples deciding not to go out on a Valentine's date, or elderly people turning down their heating, or people foregoing a holiday etc. And I felt a pang in the heart every time a professional fee invoice came in. How much sacrifice does the paying of a fee represent to our generous, self-giving people? And did the surveyors, engineers, architects, and other consultants know the true cost of their work?

Yet without these people we could go nowhere. If one sets out to build a fantastic new church centre in the heart of the community, it is impossible to do so by separating ourselves off into a hinterland bubble of amateur make-do-ism and the occasional volunteer pro bono work. At St Barnabas we had always aimed for excellence in all that we do, usually managing astonishing results with very little by way of resources. However, we had now entered a new realm, and we needed to address the huge and complex world of commercial property surrounded by the very best professionals available. Of course, we would negotiate as hard as we could to pare down every cost, and to make the scheme as economically prudent as we possibly could. Jesus himself envisaged a similar scenario, when he said: "Suppose one of you wants to build a tower. Won't you first sit down and estimate the cost to see if you have enough money to complete it?"[99] Nevertheless, while constantly testing the viability of the project, on such a large scheme we could not avoid spending very large amounts of money.

As a vicar used to signing off much more modest bills, I was fast having to readjust my perspectives. Would it all be worth it? We had set out to infiltrate the secular commercial world and carry off the prize of a new building in their midst. If we, by the grace of God, could manage to pull off this feat - you bet it would be worth it.

Project Management

Our project managers appeared to be constantly slightly behind the curve, not providing the information we needed for the project's smooth running. Demands for exhaustive reporting from the diocese were met with what was deemed to be insufficient responses from the firm we had engaged to manage the project. They were clearly floundering. Meanwhile, from my perspective, I felt that our side of the project board was overly exposed to the constant ultimatums of our diocesan partners, without adequate professional representation for our side. All of the professional team so far had been engaged as advisers to the whole project, answerable to the entire project

---

[99] Luke 14:28

board. Therefore, no one was assigned to expressly advise St Bs as we grappled with an increasingly adversarial situation in the joint project board. I wanted a skilled property professional to specifically represent us, St Bs.

The solution came ironically through a contact of Michael Bye, the Diocesan Head of Property. Heather Stanley was a structural engineer who had latterly moved specialism into project management. In the property world it is quite common for project managers to have previously worked in another construction or property area. This prior experience can give a breadth of knowledge that is helpful in giving a better understanding of the processes involved in complex property transactions. Since branching into project management, Heather had specialised in church projects. Her previous projects had included her home church: Christ Church Chislehurst, which I was familiar with having spoken there when a previous St Bs' member had become their curate. Since then, she had also done a major project in the crypt at Christ Church, Spitalfields, a grade 1 listed city church designed by the renowned English baroque architect Nicholas Hawksmoor. A project of such sensitivity would have had huge complexities which would have required an adept project manager to navigate.

We hired Heather as project director in February 2016, to work alongside the existing project managers and in particular to help in keeping the project on track with the diocese. Heather quickly grasped the full scope of the project and for the first time I felt we were being properly advised.

Within a few weeks of Heather's appointment, we started to ask the question: what were the firm retained to be project managers doing? Heather was energetically and proactively managing the project in a way that we had not seen before. Meanwhile, the supposedly main project managers seemed to be doing very little. And so, we pondered if there was anything that they were doing that Heather couldn't more ably take over? After another month it became clear that Heather should become our main project manager and that we should dispense with the services of the previous company. They were duly stood down. I liked both the partner assigned to our project and the bright young trainee who had been doing most of the leg work, and so it was a sadness to me that our engagement with them was halted so abruptly. Years later I invited them to our opening ceremony, but they declined to come, no doubt still smarting from the inevitable sourness of our professional parting.

The project to move a parish church has convoluted obscurities that no normal vicar would ever contemplate. Two major property transactions, that were completely essential for the viability of the project: the sale of the old Holden Road church and the sale of the North Wing of Solar House, and were both conditional. These had been the subject of intricate negotiations[100] with the purchasers. The developer buying our old church in Holden Road had agreed to a contract that was conditional on both him getting suitable planning permission to redevelop the church and us getting planning permission to convert Solar House. The purchaser of the North Wing at Solar House had similarly agreed to the deal being conditional on us getting planning permission to convert our end of the building

---

[100] See chapter 19.

into our new church centre. Through 2016 we proceeded with an awareness that the whole thing could come crashing down at any point. Central to that jeopardy was getting planning. Without planning the main property transactions would be void and the project would collapse. The mythical sword of Damocles[101] continued to hang over the entire project, and any progress we made, we knew could be undone in an instant. Even at this late stage, we knew that at any point the diocese could pull the plug and we would be left with nothing but a big bill for all our efforts.

However, with Heather now in charge it felt like the project had turned a corner. The Go and Grow project had had many turning points, but the appointment of Heather Stanley was particularly significant. Like the marathon runner who manages to keep going through the fabled "wall", we now felt a new energy to see the project through to its conclusion. It would not be true to say that all our problems were over; far from it. And we still had a very considerable journey ahead of us, but with Heather at the helm we never looked back.

The work continued through 2016, with ever increasing detailed design work ironing out every conceivable issue. The multifaceted nature of the project meant that effort was simultaneously required in a number of different fronts. But one pre-eminent objective loomed far above all others: obtaining planning consent. For the best part of a year, a staggering coordinated endeavour of the amazingly gifted professional team, led

---

[101] The sword of Damocles, from late Greek mythology, is a graphic description of jeopardy. According to Cicero, the sword hangs by a single horsehair above the head of the king. With great opportunity, fortune and power, comes great danger.

by Heather, was almost entirely focussed on this singular objective.

Chapter 22

Planning Permission

It was nearly two years since we had started the planning process[102] and it was now the biggest remaining obstacle that could potentially derail the entire project. The preparation for our planning application had taken endless meetings and hundreds of hours of work. Much of our work over the entirety of 2016 had been aimed at this one objective: to get planning permission. Finally, in August 2016 we heard the long-awaited news, that at last our planning application had been submitted. What a relief after all those months of preparations, with the interminable meticulous poring over details, to then be able to sit back and take a breather. The application was now with the planning authority in Barnet, and we could relax. Only we couldn't!

The planning submission, whilst a significant milestone, is not the finishing tape; this wasn't the end of the race. Go and Grow was perhaps more like the triathlon, where the moment one part of the race is completed, another equally gruelling discipline is required. So, with the Go and Grow project the milestone moment of our planning submission was like that point when the triathletes leap off their bikes and start running. You know that the final leg of the race has begun, but there is still a long way to go. There was no let-up, no relaxing. For us, this meant rounds of consultations in the lead-up to the planning committee, which was scheduled

---

[102] See chapter 12.

to consider our application towards the end of the year. We were up and running, but there was still a long way to go.

One day in September I was surprised to open a letter, addressed impersonally to The Occupier, to find that it was from me! With our planning application for Solar House submitted to Barnet planning authority we had now been consulting with the local community about the project - hence the letter. But the planning submission had signalled a noticeable change of emphasis in the Go and Grow project in other ways as well. For months we had been in a state of suspense, wondering if the project was ever going to get past the next milestone. But now, like climbing to the top of a mountain, we were able to take in the view ahead.

Most old church buildings pre-date planning conditions. Our old building, completed in 1914, was effectively free from any planning restrictions. We had the right to do whatever we deemed appropriate for the proper running of the church, only constrained by avoiding falling foul of criminality. We did not need to limit the number of people coming to church, provided we could keep everyone safe in the event of a fire. We usually set out seating for around 300 people, but on one occasion, when Brother Andrew[103] came to speak, we managed to fit in a congregation of over 600. Our people were permitted to park their cars anywhere that it was legal to park in the local vicinity, and there was never any suggestion that we should be held to account for this.

---

[103] Brother Andrew is author of the best-selling book: God's smuggler and founder of Open Doors. This extraordinary man is one of the most revered Christians in recent history and it was one of the greatest privileges of my life to host him at St Bs.

But the moment one applies for a new planning consent, either to extend one's existing building, or as in our case, to relocate to a new building, then one becomes obligated to comply to the full rigours of modern planning regulations. Many rail against this exponential growth of red tape, but these regulations are put there in order to better care for the variety of needs of the community. In particular, planning regulations are intended to protect the weak and the voiceless against powerful institutions. Often big businesses, driven by financial gain, can seek to do inappropriate developments that are destructive to a local area. The planning process, and ensuing regulations and conditions, are there to protect the general public.

For most of my career, I have thought of myself as the underdog, an heroic David striding out to fell the gigantic Goliath.[104] The Go and Grow project itself had been, from its inception, a battle against near-impossible odds. Of course, I was aware that such a self-view would be susceptible to vanity and could quickly lead to delusion and tilting at windmills.[105] But part of both our ecclesiology and missiology was to see ourselves as a counterculture, a beachhead for the Kingdom of God in a hostile land.

When Jesus came to earth, he did so in the most remarkable way. He didn't come to the corridors of power or hobnob with the great and good. He didn't leverage influence through writing books, commanding armies or taking over municipalities. He didn't target the main centres of the ancient world: Rome, Alexandria, Athens. Instead, he grew up in a very ordinary family living in a

---

[104] 1 Samuel 17.
[105] Cervantes fabled Don Quixote hallucinated that windmills were giants for him as a gallant knight to do battle with.

tiny village in a forgotten backwater at the far reaches of the Roman Empire. Given the choice between the senate and marketplace, Jesus would always be found in the latter. He associated with ordinary fishermen and the like. He travelled on foot, but never very far.

Jesus ran his campaign to save the world on completely different principles to those we are familiar with in our frenetic, competitive, commercialised world. He was intent on reaching out to people, not despite their ordinariness, but because of it. For all this we see him as far more 'real' than the great movers and shakers of history, as he somehow connected with the soft underbelly of humanity. Jesus was God incarnate; God fleshed out amongst us. How do we follow his example? How do we live in an incarnational way?

We had had ongoing consultations with our own membership, but now this had to be broadened out. The project became the subject of intricately planned consultations, using a professional communication consultant. These were conducted, not just to communicate our vision, but as a legal requirement for the process of running up to getting planning permission. The consultations were aimed beyond the membership of St Barnabas, at other stakeholders and the local community. They involved letters sent out, special meetings, big infographics and feedback surveys. The response to the consultations would be crucial.

Very often people who would never darken the door of the church for worship, still have a strong sense of ownership of historic parish church buildings. These local residents would not come at the subject from a faith perspective and would not understand the missional reasons for the project, but rather would be invested in the preservation of a local landmark.

The local residents who were raising the objections, were seen as the valiant little guy, fighting for his or her rights against the St Barnabas ogre. I was still clinging to my identity as the brave underdog, desperately wanting to follow Jesus by leading a grass-roots movement, far from the corridors of power. Yet I was now faced with the prospect of being styled as something very different: a big institution set on trashing the local area for our own selfish motives. This turning of the tables sat very uncomfortably with me.

The end of 2016 came and went and still the planning committee hadn't discussed our project. The delays were frustrating, but in the new year of 2017 we were finally greeted with a planning committee date and the shadow of the looming planning decision. This had been over two years in the making. The first pre-app meeting with Barnet's principal planning officer was distant memory from March 2015. But now, in early 2017, we faced the prospect of the Barnet Planning Committee deliberating and ruling on our project. Like so many hurdles that we had overcome before, this was to be another make or break moment.

Up to this point we had mainly dealt with the professional planners at Barnet. But a planning committee is made up, not of professionals, but of politicians. Having dispensed their advice, the professional planners withdrew into the background, deferring to their political overlords. However, these local councillors are far from inexperienced, many of them having sat on planning committees for years and gained considerable expertise and proficiency in planning matters. We were not dealing with amateurs, and it would be impossible to pull the wool over their eyes. Nevertheless, local politicians are motivated by fundamentally different principles to that of the professional planning officers. Irrespective of the rationality of a planning application and its adherence to all the district's defined planning objectives, the views of local voters would ultimately be the most persuasive voice in each councillor's ears.

In the run up to the Planning Committee I had met with a couple of local councillors to make our case. Whilst they were both sympathetic and courteous, they had made it very clear to me that they had major concerns. It was evident that their mailbox had been inundated with protestations about our proposed move to the High Road. The biggest complaint was about traffic and parking.

The date of the Planning Committee was set for Wednesday 29th March 2017. It was to take place at Hendon Town Hall, a magnificent throwback to a time when local government was split up into suburban towns, now all subsumed into the amorphous mass of the humongous Borough of Barnet. Hendon Town Hall is now surrounded by the incredible Middlesex University campus, where a £200m building investment has produced a major centre for learning in North London. This last vestige of a bygone age stands proud and resilient to change, at least for the time being.

Planning Committees are open meetings where the public are permitted to come and observe. Sometimes a committee decision can be influenced by perceived support in the room. We wanted to show that this project was well supported by our membership, so I had encouraged as many members of St Barnabas as possible to come and support the application hearing.

About seventy St Bs members turned up and we initially gathered in the rather cramped ground floor foyer. There was also a small group of local residents who had come to object and were clearly rattled by our overbearing presence. The old building was not ideally suited to accommodate such large numbers of people and the atmosphere was tense. It was unclear whether the committee room would be large enough to fit all of us, so when we were eventually invited to go upstairs to the meeting, those who were pre-booked to speak, either for or against the project, were asked to go first. That included me and some of the local residents. I suddenly felt very alone. This isolation didn't last long, and the frosty officialdom descended into a happy chaos as everyone else bustled into the room.

The committee hearing was in a long, relatively thin upstairs hall, with the committee of local councillors arrayed around a rectangle of tables at one end and a congregation of the public in rows of chairs at the other. The committee had a list of applications to consider, but as far as I could tell only ours was the subject of interest to the gathered group in the public seats. We all sat stoically through a series of agenda items of no interest to any of us.

Then at last it was our turn. Our planning consultant, Barry, gave a clear case for why this was a reasonable project. I was then asked to speak. I had been briefed that I had no more than three minutes and that if I overran the chair would cut me off. Such timing is difficult for a preacher, so I had meticulously prepared my speech, practiced it and timed it. My objective was to explain our

Pic 22.1 The planning committee in session on 29th March 2017, from spectators' view.

vision for the project in terms that were understandable and able to be embraced by this secular committee. I laid out the five dimensions of Go and Grow and how this could impact North Finchley for the better. And finally, I addressed the concerns about parking head on, saying that we were committed to getting our membership to park in local car parks, rather than clogging up the neighbouring streets. My time was up, but I had managed to finish with a couple of seconds to spare. Relieved but still nervy, I sat down.

Various local residents then spoke in objection. One exasperated local quoted our own figures saying: "It's ridiculous, thousands of people coming to this building in a residential area." One of our over enthusiastic supporters at the back shouted "Amen", but at that moment I just wanted them to keep quiet. The numbers were based on us applying for ultimately having up to seven services on a Sunday, each with up to 700 attendees. A total of 4,900 sounded terrifying for a local resident used to being able to park outside his or her own home. Of course, we were nowhere near that number, with our four services rarely getting beyond a combined total of 700 or 800 including youth and children. But no amount of telling our neighbours not to worry, would appease their sense of dread.

During the proceedings the committee members could question those who had come to speak. One of the committee members turned to me and asked: "What is your plan B?" I responded: "Faith is not having a plan B." This momentarily confounded her as she mumbled, half to herself, "Not my faith."

The chairman drew the discussion to a close and asked for a vote. We all held our breath. There was nothing more we could do now. The chair called for those in favour, and counted: one, two, three, four, five, six. I thought there were twelve on the committee, so still I didn't know if it was to be carried. Then those against: one, two, three, four, five, silence. The chair addressed the committee: "So that is passed."

The rest of what he said was drowned out as a great cheer went up from the St Barnabas throng. People were on their feet, laughing and applauding and hugging each other. I saw the angry faces of the local residents' group as they abruptly walked out, but this was not a moment for pacification; that would come later. We had won by the narrowest of margins: just one vote, and victory was sweet. Faced with this eruption of joy, the chair called for a break in the proceedings, to allow the hubbub to slacken off. The St Bs horde filed out of the room, leaving the committee to its ongoing business. Happy chatter, back-slapping and smiles accompanied us down the grand

Pic 22.2 At Hendon Town Hall, just after we had received approval.

stairs of the town hall. Near the bottom, I called for quiet and led us in an impromptu prayer of thanksgiving. A glow of triumph surrounded us; beyond all expectations this extraordinary project was really going to happen.[106]

---

[106] The planning consent was still at this point subject to a six-week judicial review period, during which a potential legal challenge could be mounted. In the event no such challenge emerged, and the planning decision was ratified.

Chapter 23
Construction, constriction and completion

Tender documents for the construction project to convert Solar House into our new church centre had been prepared at the latter end of 2016. This was inevitably slightly speculative as it came before we had actual planning permission, but such is the time-lag in these matters that it was necessary to do this work in advance in order to meet future timescales.

This was just for phase 1 of the project, which excluded the new auditorium on the back and the so called "orangery" on the front. However, this was still to be a major construction project and it included massive external works around our fantastic new entrance, a new lift and a new staircase. In addition, on the roof we were to fit an astonishing 80m^2 of solar panels[107] which, combined with new energy-saving LED lighting largely switched by PIR motion sensors, would enable us to have an environmental rating of "very good." Inside the layout would be modified with a considerable number of new walls and new doors. There would be three new kitchens, including a commercial kitchen on the ground floor, adjacent to the fully fitted café bar overlooking the foyer area. The toilets would result in us having a total of 26 cubicles, 28 sinks, 10 urinals, 3 showers and 3 disabled

---

[107] The area of solar panels on our roof should produce in the order of 10,000kwh per year.

toilets. The whole place would be redecorated, and the majority of the floor coverings would be renewed. There would also be a small amount of structural reinforcement to the ground floor slab.[108] Finally, in front of the building, a garden would be planted, including a large Christmas tree, and a church bell would be fixed above the main entrance. Once professional fees and VAT had been allowed for, the cost of the construction contract would be in the order of £3m.

Three contractors submitted tenders and the stand-out submission was from a well-respected company: Russell Cawberry. They were duly engaged, and in the autumn of 2017, work started on converting the building. To mark the occasion, we had a ground-breaking ceremony, on Thursday 16th of November 2017. The invitation list included: the Bishop of Edmonton,[109] members of the project board, the contractors, several of our professional team, key leaders from within the church and various local dignitaries. We took all the guests up to the first floor where we had set everything out in readiness. We started with some sung worship and some prayers. Then a ceremonial sledgehammer was brought out and Bishop Rob, myself and Heather Stanley each took a swing at a designated wall. Afterwards, other guests came and joined in the destruction. Dave Harvey our facilities coordinator, a burly builder, took one swing at the wall and it totally collapsed with a thundering crash, bringing the smashing episode to a timely end. Sparkling wine flowed and we enjoyed this moment of visible progress being made.

---

[108] See chapter 13.
[109] Rt Revd Rob Wickham, Bishop of Edmonton.

Pic 23.1 Ground-breaking ceremony. Right to left: Bishop
Rob Wickham, Richard Greeves, Michael Bye, and me.

Pic 23.2 Me taking a sledge-hammer to a wall.

The demands of a large construction project are a little bit like that of a hungry baby. At any point, the newborn construction scheme might start to cry to be fed with intricate specification details of what we would like. Working drawings are highly detailed and specify almost everything, but inevitably once on the ground, builders need additional details of things that have either changed or not been fully specified: the colour and style inside the lifts, the position of light switches, the design of "manifestations"[110] on the glass doors. We engaged qualified accountant Sarah Restall as our change manager to field these incessant demands. Sarah was a committed member of the church and already our long-standing treasurer, so she was fully conversant with the project. She brought a level of scrutiny to the subject that I believed would be a pivotal factor in its success.

Such was the complexity of the legal property transactions that, whilst we had exchanged contracts on the sale of the old church building, we had made allowance for us to remain in occupation until September 2018, when the newly converted Solar House would be available for us to move into. The developer, whom we had known as "Paradigm", had contracted to buy the property in the name of a previously unknown company called "Cullen and Davis 2 Ltd". Despite being signed and deposit paid, the contract had elements that meant we were still not completely certain if the deal would go ahead. These conditional elements were called a "unilateral notice."

---

[110] These are the translucent etchings that are a safety requirement of large expanses of glass, to stop people bumping into them.

We now had builders working up at Solar House, and so had clearly long passed the point of no return. We therefore wanted the last remaining uncertainty settled and asked that the unilateral notice be removed. The developer procrastinated. We got our lawyers to take up the issue with their counterparts, but to no avail. The developer was resisting all our moves to ratify the contract. At this point the developer had only paid a relatively small deposit, so whilst we had some money in the bank, it was a long way short of what we needed to complete the project. The rest of our spiralling debts were still being bank-rolled by the diocese.

However, the contract for sale of the old church had a completion date in it, at which point the remaining monies should be paid and the ownership of our old church would pass to the developer. This in turn would trigger a short-term lease back to us, to enable us to remain in occupation until the move. I felt reasonably relaxed, that despite the developer's stalling and obfuscation, all would come good on completion day. As it turned out, this feeling of assurance was a false hope.

The completion date came and went without them completing. I was incredulous! In my previous career I had overseen hundreds of property transactions and had never previously come across an intentionally delayed completion; in my experience it simply never happened. I assumed that the developer was now in breach of contract. We asked our lawyers how they could get away with this. It was explained to me that completion dates in real property contracts are not "of the essence" in English law. In other words, missing the completion date doesn't automatically void the contract. We didn't know what was going on. Why was the developer dawdling? They claimed to have the money ready and waiting, but we couldn't help fear that they might be facing insolvency; what other possible reason could there be for the delay? We got our lawyers to issue a notice to complete.

As the date of the notice to complete approached there still appeared to be no movement. Angry emails were exchanged, and it became impossible to tell who was calling whose bluff. In the end, at the very last minute, like Indiana Jones snatching his hat from under the closing portcullis, the developers completed. The money arrived and our jangled nerves calmed once more. I still don't know why they pushed us to the final deadline, but none of that matters now. Frustratingly, our disputes with the developer were not over, and the next area of contention would be to do with a beautiful window.

Memorials and other artefacts

Moving from an historic old church building meant that there were an enormous number of objects to be sorted through. Thankfully we had removed our old organ some years previously and sold off our unused old oak pulpit.[111] But there remained huge quantities of objects, most of which were in poor condition and left unused for decades; relics of a bye-gone age. The vast majority of these had little intrinsic value and had to be disposed of or sold on Ebay. However, there were a number of pieces that were significant. Some we were keen to take with us. The moveable stuff was relatively easy to organise: fine

---

[111] Both of these arrangements required what is called a "faculty", which is a Church of England permission given by the Diocesan Advisory Committee (DAC).

oak furniture, a small stone font, the royal coat of arms and so on.

However, memorials need to be treated in quite a different way. These are artefacts that have invariably been given by relatives in memory of someone deeply loved. Two candle style lamps were given by a former church member in memory of his parents, and we were able to arrange for them to be returned to him. But the donors of some of the older brass wall plaques were more difficult to trace and so we simply organised to take these with us, and they have subsequently been re-fixed to the walls on the main staircase half-landing in our new building.

The main memorial in our old building was a spectacular carved oak screen which acted as the entrance into the side chapel. On either side of the entrance were listed those local lads who had died in service of their country in the First World War. The list is very poignant, tragically with repeated names denoting two or three sons of the same family. One notable name is that of Private John Parr, who died just after his seventeenth birthday, having lied about his age when he joined up. He is documented as the first Tommy to die on the Western Front. As this memorial screen was not structural, we reasoned that it was a chattel and could be removed.

The screen was nearly 4m high and we quickly realised that there would be only one place in the new church where the ceiling height would be sufficient to accommodate it: the staircase. The screen was designed to be walked through as an entrance archway. But we were now going to be fixing it to a wall. I reasoned that for it to look appropriate in that siting, we would need to design something to go on the wall behind it. Therefore, we commissioned church member and artist, Joy Girvin, to paint a mural of a poppy field to go behind the screen. Joy was an exhibiting artist specialising in garden scenes. Her bright palette of colours and freestyle of painting perhaps made her not the most obvious choice for the sombre subject of a war memorial mural. But, inspired by the poppy display at the Tower of London[112] for the year of the hundredth anniversary of the Armistice, she produced this amazing scene that perfectly complements the rich carving of the screen. The screen and mural behind it were finally unveiled at our Remembrance Sunday service at 11.00 am on 11th November 2018, exactly 100 years to the minute from the Armistice that ended the Great War.

Pic 23.3 Unveiling of the war memorial screen mural.

It transpires that a parish church doesn't need to have a cross on top of it, but it does need a bell! Under Ecclesiastical Law, Canon F16 states that for it to be a parish church it is necessary to install a bell which can be rung to call people to divine worship. As far as I know there is no requirement to actually ring the bell and, as a church we had only very rarely used our bell at the old building, generally at Easter. With the requirement to have a bell we naturally looked at moving our existing one. The bell was hung in its own brick turret on top of the roof at a very inaccessible point. It soon became clear that the cost of taking it down would be astronomic, requiring a lot of scaffolding. So instead, we looked to see if we could buy a second-hand bell to replace it and found that they are readily available. A bell was acquired and given to the contractors to install above the new entrance, with a remotely controlled electronic clapper.

Most difficult of all the artefacts from the old building were the windows. The old St Barnabas had some fine stained-glass windows. It was impossible for us to take all of these, but two in particular were singled out for removal and refitting as back-lit art pieces in the new building. One of these was a small casement window depicting St Barnabas. This delightful little window was rarely seen by regular members of St Bs as it was tucked away in an obscure small room adjacent to the balcony. However, I had enjoyed it for many years, when this room had been my office. The removal of it was a simple matter of replacing the hinged casement. This we duly did and took it with us.

The other window destined for moving with us was an altogether more complicated affair. It was the enormous main east window, which had been installed after the

Second World War as a war memorial with the inscription: "TO THE GLORY OF GOD, A THANK OFFERING FOR PRESERVATION AND VICTORY 1939-45." The window, in a post-pre-Raphaelite style, depicts the resurrected Jesus flanked by two archangels looking down at six disciples (two of them women) along with the two angels they met at the tomb. [113] Early on in the project, I had had a discussion with the Queen's Deputy Lieutenant [114] for Barnet: Martin Russell. Martin was a zealous advocate for war memorials in the area, and when our move became a known possibility, he took a great interest in helping with arrangements for our various memorials. Martin put me in touch with a local stained glass window specialist, the aptly named Matthew Lloyd-Winder.

The removal of the main war memorial east window was written into the project and so became a condition of the planning consent to convert the church into luxury apartments. The developer had to ensure that the window be moved somewhere where it could be viewed by the public. We had volunteered to house the window in our new church premises, and whilst we could not insist on it coming to us if the developer could find an alternative site for public display, we were the obvious choice. We had also offered to pay for a good proportion of the removal, restoration and reinstatement. This was surely an offer too good to refuse, and it was written into our contract with the developer.

Once the property had exchanged contracts, whilst we were still the legal owners, we were not permitted to make

---

[113] Luke 24:4.
[114] Representative of the Queen for the borough of Barnet.

material alterations to it. So, we asked the developer for permission to remove the window. We heard nothing. We pressed for an answer. Still no permission. Without explicit permission we were not legally entitled to do the removal works, so frustratingly we couldn't touch it. This impasse went on for months, until eventually the time for our move came and we had to walk away from our old building leaving our precious war memorial window behind us to an uncertain fate.

We may never know why the developer had obstructed the removal of the window, but one theory has to do with CIL.[115] CIL payments are conditions of planning consent and are the means by which developers are required to contribute to necessary local infrastructure. Residential developments cause the local population to increase, which in turn leads to the need for more schools, medical clinics, and roads. CIL payments allow local authorities to get the developers to pay their fair share of this burden to the local economy. They are often very large and can be one of the major expenses of a development project. It is possible that the developer of the old St Barnabas church thought that the removal of the main east window would be a work of sufficient proportion to be deemed a partial implementation of the planning permission, thereby triggering their CIL payment to Barnet. Refusal to let us touch the window was therefore a simple cheap way to delay having to pay out hundreds of thousands of pounds.

From our side, the refusal to let us remove the window put us through untold anxiety about one of our greatest treasures. At the move, we were forced to walk away and leave the window to become the sole responsibility of the

---

[115] Community infrastructure levy.

developer. Eventually, the window was taken out, at the developer's cost, by our friend Matthew Lloyd-Winder, and restored at his Hertfordshire workshop. Matthew was a classic artisan craftsman; a genius with glass who it was a joy to have work for us. The window was finally installed in the lower ground floor foyer of our new building, one of the few places where the ceiling height could be made high enough to accommodate it, and where it now looks spectacular. It was unveiled there at our Remembrance Sunday service in November 2019, over a year after we had moved in. Better late than never.

Chapter 24
Arrival

The Go and Grow project was an adventure that lifted a generation of St Bs to great heights of faith. What a privilege it has been for me to lead a church like this. Unconcerned for their own well-being, the St Bs membership strained at the oars of missional endeavour as if their life depended on it. The move conjured up inspiring levels of commitment to the cause. As such, it has been of great benefit to the level of dedication and discipleship within the church. However, that is not the full story; there is a darker shadow side that has also left its mark.

The true cost of the Go and Grow project should not just be measured in financial terms. The relentless strain of the project took its toll on all of us who were involved. Along the way we had had numbers of the professional team back out. Of the original project board, apart from me, only two others, Hannah Parker and Andrew Garwood Watkins, managed to endure through to the conclusion. Hannah, an accountant and faithful St Bs member, was instrumental in putting together and maintaining the business plan for the project. Apart from our myriad meetings, she also spent endless hours in these spreadsheet preparations. Her lucid pragmatism combined with resilient faith was a key factor in the project's success. Andrew, a property professional, was a volunteer who freely offered his services to the diocese. He ended up as the project board's chair and brought the sharpest professionalism I've ever encountered to our proceedings. At times terrifying, his commitment to the cause was ultimately borne out by his staggering investment of time.

Then there was the collective burden borne by the St Bs PCC,[116] as we laboured for endless hours, stepping out in high-stakes faith in ways rarely expected in local church governance. Depending on when one dates the start of the project, this was strictly speaking the work of, not one, but at least seven PCCs. These involved a total of 51 people, including 9 who served for the entire duration of the project. In particular, during the pivotal years of 2014-2017, the PCC was truly heroic and will last long in my memory as the most faith-filled committee on which I have ever had the privilege to serve.[117]

In hindsight, the toll borne by the St Bs staff is perhaps the biggest deficit of all. During the project, I had to step back from some of the more day to day duties of staff management and oversight. In turn, others had to step up and take on greater responsibility and sometimes this onerous burden was difficult to carry. Then as the move

---

[116] Parochial Church Council.

[117] The PCC 'hall of fame' over the years from 2014-2018 included: Revd. Henry Kendal (Vicar, Chair and Project Board Member), Sam Markey (Churchwarden, Vice-Chair and Project Board Member), Nikki Marfleet (Churchwarden), Margaret Peach (Secretary), Hannah Parker (Project Board Member), Sarah Restall (Treasurer), Mike Vamvadelis (who attended Project Board meetings), Revd. Chris Alexander, Alice Atashkar, Bella Barnum-Bobb, Shirley Boateng, Elizabeth Boreham, Revd. Colin Brookes, Revd. David Brown, Vivienne Burgon, Jonathan Burnett, Ros Hoare, Elliott Ireton, Mark Johnson, Bill Knock, Virginia Knox, Jan Kovar, Fraser Mackay, Zengani Mhone, Revd. Mike Pavlou, Neil Richards, Revd. Helen Shannon, Ryan Venn-Dunn, David Vincent, Tom Wheatley, Kate Wong, and Andy Yeates.

itself approached, the intensity of work increased to fever pitch levels as every tiny detail of church life needed to be poured over, pruned down to its bare essentials, and packed up into a transportable bundle. Things that had been embedded into our culture for generations were unceremoniously dispensed with. The totality of the reorganisation of our ministries permeated every sinew of our church body. Those fielding this monumental effort were left utterly exhausted.

In the couple of years since the move, after many years of incredible longevity of staff deployment, astonishingly we have seen an almost complete turnover of our staff team. Apart from Dave Harvey, who remains a fixture in our operations department, only Peter Troup has been on staff since before the move, and Peter himself only joined the staff in the latter stages of the project. I remain one of only two pastors, out of fifteen, still serving at the church, who has been around long enough to predate the start of the construction project just four years ago.[118] As I write this, I am myself preparing to move on from St Bs in just six months' time. Why such attrition? It would be wrong to ascribe all causation of this haemorrhage to Go and Grow, as the COVID19 pandemic probably played an even more significant role in prompting people to move on, but there is no doubt that Go and Grow played its part. It seems strange that those who worked so hard to fulfil such an incredible achievement would then move on so quickly after its culmination. At the very point where the project is set to bear fruit, those who fought so courageously to gain that prize have chosen to leave. And yet a different set of skills is required in peacetime to

---

[118] At the time of writing – autumn 2021.

those needed through a war.[119] So, it seems that those of us who have emerged from the years of battling feel our job at St Bs is now complete. The time has come for us to bow out and allow our successors to pick up the baton, with an array of exciting new opportunities in front of them. Meanwhile, the battle-weary heroes of the former foray have moved on to other campaigns. They will carry with them invaluable and hard-won experience which will equip them for the future in a way that no amount of training ever could. They possess a sword forged in the red-hot crucible of Go and Grow.

The Move

As the summer of 2018 approached, the arrangements for the move were thought out in incredible detail by our Change Manager, Sarah Restall. Each ministry of the church was responsible for packing up their own equipment. Huge amounts of obsolete detritus had to be disposed of, as everyone engaged in a momentous clear-out. One of the 'sons' of a family removal company, was a St Bs member, and they offered us a competitive quote. Now the time had arrived. We had sold our old church, but had leased it back in order to stay in occupation until the move, so we had fixed dates to work to.

The Office moved first, shifting all the equipment up to the High Road early in August, so that we could get our operations up and running in good time. Then, three weeks later, the final move took place. The old church was

---

[119] The British electorate famously voted out the heroic war-time Prime Minister Winston Churchill, in favour of a new peacetime Labour government led by Clement Attlee in 1945.

Pic 24.1 Poster announcing our
move that was displayed at
Woodside Park Station.

emptied of everything and left as a magnificent echoing, hollow shell. Meanwhile, up at the High Road boxes were directed to pre-labelled destinations throughout our new extensive four-floor church centre, in an operation of military proficiency. One venue took on a sublime tranquillity, while the other became a hubbub of movement and endeavour.

The final Sunday in the old church took place in an empty building. No chairs, no PA system, no literature and no adornments. But, far from being a barren experience something truly wonderful happened as we started worshipping to a single acoustic guitar. The vacant space was alluring to movement and, unprompted, people all over the building started to dance before the Lord. Flags were waving in every direction in a glorious, spontaneous celebration of all that God had done for us. I looked around with amazement at such expressions of unbridled joy. It made me wonder why we had not gotten rid of all our clutter before – who needs chairs?

The following Sunday, 9th September 2018, we gathered outside the front of the old church for the last time. The doors were locked as we had now surrendered occupation to the developers; this was no longer our building. With stewards, banners and a portable PA system on a backpack, we had planned a procession from the old to the new. I had wondered how many would turn up, knowing that St Bs was notoriously bad at joining anything that was out of routine. I was hoping that at least 50 would show up, otherwise, it would go down as an embarrassing damp squib. In the event, 350 people arrived, spilling out over the forecourt and pavement. The weather was mercifully fine, and this joyous throng set off on the just under a mile parade. We soon spread out over a couple of hundred metres, as the vanguard strode out and the stragglers tarried at the rear. The whole event took on the style of a pageant and many local people stopped and watched the jubilant spectacle.

Pic 24.2 The procession leaving the old St Barnabas building.

Pic 24.3 The procession arriving at the new building.

When 20 minutes later we arrived at the High Road, I was amazed to be greeted by another couple of hundred people who had chosen to be the welcoming delegation. In scenes that I imagine might be a bit like Jesus riding into Jerusalem on Palm Sunday, the bell was ringing, flags were waving, and onlookers came out of shops, opened their front doors and hung over their balconies. After leading a prayer from the top of the steps, I encouraged everyone to go into the packed ground floor of our ñew church. The service was a thrill of excitement. I preached a short sermon, which I doubt anyone heard. We were like children with a new toy.

Pic 24.4 First Sunday in the new building.

Two weeks after the great procession Bishop Rob Wickham,[120] our local bishop, who had shown generous friendship as a staunch supporter of the project, came to licence the new building. It is still possible for parish churches to be consecrated, however, it was decided that our building, probably because it is out of the ordinary, would be licensed instead. I was delighted with this decision because as far as I can tell there is no advantage for a parish church to be consecrated over being licensed. A licensed parish church can fulfil everything a consecrated building can, and yet falls outside the jurisdiction of great swathes of Church of England bureaucracy. So, this simple legal circumvention has set St Bs free to determine how our own building is shaped,

---

[120] The Bishop of Edmonton.

without fear of breaching red-tape and incurring ecclesiastical reprimands for failures in compliance.

The ceremony was to start with the Bishop, in full episcopal robes, taking his crook and banging on the front doors of the new church. However, as Bishop Rob moved to knock on the doors, they automatically slid open, leaving him standing there, crook in hand, but with nothing but open space in front of him. We all dissolved into laughter. Once through the doors, Rob knelt on the floor just inside the entrance and with a great theatrical flourish drew in chalk on the floor an Alpha and Omega, to dedicate the building to our God, who is over everything and knows the beginning from the end. The service continued as a fantastic act of worship and praise to God for the astonishing provision of this place.

Having taken advice from others who have undertaken large building projects, we had decided to delay the official opening of the building until we had worked through initial teething issues. This was good advice, as the first couple of months were full of unforeseen glitches that needed resolving. These included working out how the security worked. At the start, one of the maglocks was installed in the wrong direction, with the result that people were getting trapped in the lift foyer unable to escape. Once we discovered this, after consoling a distressed captive, we switched this lock off until it had been reversed and the problem solved. We very quickly realised that this new building was different in kind to the old one. The old St Bs was a basic shell with very little sophistication. The new building had multiple moving parts, four floors all relating differently to one another, security, air handling and computer controls for all sorts of refinements. It was going to take some time to get used to it.

The official opening was set for 5pm on Sunday 13th January 2019, four months after the move. The relatively new Bishop of London, The Rt Revd and Rt Hon Dame Sarah Mullally,[121] was invited, as was a return visit by our local bishop The Rt Revd Rob Wickham. I had invited many people who had been involved with the project over the years, together with some members of my family.

The day fell on my brother's birthday, which had also been my late father's birthday (he would've been 99). So, it had a family poignancy for us. I had invited my 93-year-old mother, expecting that she would politely decline. Therefore, it came as a surprise that she announced she would be coming. My mother, who had frustratingly lost her sight some years before, was by this time living in a granny-annexe at my sister's house just outside Nottingham. Increasingly frail, she rarely travelled, so it was with great excitement that arrangements were made for her to attend the ceremony. Because of the tremendous pains taken to bring my mother to the event, no one was in any doubt who was the principal guest of honour. Bishop Sarah was one of the first to take the opportunity to come and greet my much-venerated mother, who revelled in the occasion. To this day, this was the last time she has ventured beyond the immediate vicinity of her home.

Only in retrospect will we know what events and achievements in our lives have lasting significance and I suspect that my crowning glory will not be achieving the

---

[121] Bishop Sarah was made Bishop of London on 8th March 2018 and assumed office on 24th May 2018.

Go and Grow project, but being married to Jane and being father to our children. Nevertheless, I was aware that this moment was a special milestone, the like of which are rare in a lifespan. So it was very precious that my mother was there with me on that momentous occasion.

Pic 24.5 Official opening with Bishop Sarah Mullally, in front of the "Barnabas" window.

It was a fantastic worship service. The Bishop duly pulled the string to open the curtains revealing the diminutive Barnabas window and a small plaque commemorating the occasion. Bishop Sarah prayed, preached and blessed us. And afterwards we had the obligatory buffet with sparkling wine. I was able to thank our Architect, our Project Manager, our friends from the diocese and any number of the incredible team that had gone above and beyond to realise this dream. For some years I had benefitted from having an executive coach to help me through some of the most testing periods of my ministry, and it was thrilling that she and her husband were able to attend. After all was done, we returned home exhausted and happy to share time and pizza with our family.

The journey is not over. Phase two: the building of the main auditorium, lies tantalizingly ahead of St Bs. It will be yet another adventure of faith as the church sets out to fulfil a great vision with no resources available to do so. Yet I have no doubt it will be fulfilled, as God has promised, in His perfect timing. It is of course not a stage of the journey that I will be part of. From the beginning, I have been aware that this project was and is bigger than me. Famously the architect Antonio Gaudi, when starting the construction of the Basilica de la Sagrada Família[122] in Barcelona in 1882, knew that the project would outlive him. It was finally due for completion in 2026,[123] 100 years after Gaudi's death. Thankfully, St Barnabas is not on the same scale, and hopefully, the timescales for completion will be much shorter, but the principle is still true. We do not build these things for ourselves, but for those who come after us.

---

[122] Despite its gargantuan size, Sagrada Família is actually just a local church, consecrated as a basilica by the Pope in 2010.
[123] This has now been delayed still further by the COVID19 pandemic.

Pic 24.6 CGI depiction of phase two, the 500-seat new church auditorium.

The opportunities for St Bs to break new ground for the kingdom are countless. And those of us who are leaving do so with a huge sense of satisfaction that we have been involved in achieving something incredible for that future harvest. The last two decades have been a startling adventure. Often with great trepidation, we elected to take the rollercoaster of abandoned faith, rather than a make-do compromise. Rather than settle for comfortable mediocracy, St Bs chose, if not quite the fabled nuclear option, most certainly the Solar option.

Photo/image credits

The vast majority of the images used are from the St Bs archive or taken by the author. Where known, the originator is also credited.

Front cover	Ian Mitchell. http://www.ianmitchellillustrator.com/
Pic 1.1	Interior of St Bs - original photo taken by Shu Tomioka.
Pic 2.1	From original fundraising Brochure for St Barnabas (1914), St Bs's archive.
Pic 2.2	John and Anne Coles, Original John Coles.
Pic 3.1	St Barnabas, Holden Road, St Bs archive.
Pic 3.2	David Gurtler's report, original David Gurtler.
Pic 3.3	Churches by architect John Samuel Alder, original David Gurtler.
Pic 4.1	Hagia Sophia, Istanbul, Henry Kendal
Pic 4.2	Santa Sabina, Rome, Henry Kendal.
Pic 4.3	Lady Chapel, Ely Cathedral, Henry Kendal.
Pic 4.4	Liverpool's two Cathedrals. Henry Kendal.
Pic 5.1	Marc's elevation, Original Marc Rawcliffe.
Pic 5.2	TFL site adjacent to station, St Bs archive.
Pic 5.3	Ian Mitchell's cartoon in church magazine, St Bs archive, original Ian Mitchell.
Pic 5.4	Parish map, original taken from London Diocese website.
Pic 5.5	Bishop Peter Wheatley, St Bs archive.
Pic 6.1	Dorchester Group site, High Road between North Finchley and Whetstone, Henry Kendal.
Pic 6.2	Old Furnitureland site, North Finchley High Road, Henry Kendal.
Pic 7.1	Solar House, Henry Kendal.

Printed in Great Britain
by Amazon